BOB WOOLMER ON
BOWLING

Bob Woolmer

Tim Noakes

with Helen Moffett

NEW
HOLLAND

This edition first published in 2010 by New Holland Publishers (UK) Ltd
London • Cape Town • Sydney • Auckland
www.newhollandpublishers.com

Garfield House, 86–88 Edgware Road, London W2 2EA, United Kingdom
Cornelis Struik House, 80 McKenzie Street, Cape Town 8001, South Africa
Unit 1, 66 Gibbes Street, Chatswood, NSW 2067, Australia
218 Lake Road, Northcote, Auckland, New Zealand

New Holland Publishing is a member of Avusa Ltd

Extracted from the title *Bob Woomer's Art and Science of Cricket*

Reproduction by Hirt & Carter Cape (Pty) Ltd
Printed and bound by Replika Press Pvt Ltd, India

10 9 8 7 6 5 4 3 2 1

Publishing Manager: Linda de Villiers
Editor and Content Consultant: Tom Eaton
Designer: Beverley Dodd
Cover Designer: Neal Cobourne
Principal Photographer: Carl Fourie
Bowling Grips Illustrator: James Berrangé
Technical Illustrators: James Berrangé and Martin Jones
Proofreaders: Roxanne Reid, Anthony Sharpe and Joy Clack
Indexer: Dawn Dobbins

ISBN: 978 1 84773 750 2

Front cover image © CARL COURT/epa/Corbis
Back cover image © Graham Chadwick/Allsport

The authors gratefully acknowledge permission to use copyrighted material from the following: Kerith Aginsky, Justin Durandt, Gallo Images/Getty Images, Janine Gray, Paul Hurrion, Brian Kantor, Alan Knott, Peter Philpott, Marc Portus, Quintic Consultancy Ltd, Martin Schwellnus and Richard Stretch. It has not been possible to trace all copyright holders.

Please contact the publishers at the above address in case of errors or omissions.

CONTENTS

Introduction   4

    A Brief History of Bowling   5

The Basic Action   8

    The Dangers of a Mixed Action   11

    Bowling off the Wrong Foot   12

    The Run-Up   14

    Throwing   22

    Rhythm and Accuracy   37

    Line and Length   40

Medium-Pace and Fast Bowling   46

    Creating a Monster: The Fast Bowler   48

    The Deliveries   51

    The Science of Swing   69

Slow Bowling   85

    The Basic Principles of Spin   88

    The Art of Deceit   90

    The Deliveries   92

    Finger-Spin   93

    The Aerodynamics of Spin and the Magnus Effect   101

    Wrist-Spin   108

    Shane Warne: The Best Wrist-Spinner of all Time?   116

    And the Last Word Goes to Clarrie Grimmett   119

Select Bibliography   122

Index   126

INTRODUCTION

Opening batsmen who faced the pace attacks of the West Indies or Australia in the 1970s will look grim as they recall harrowing half-hours, or show off scars and crooked fingers, insisting that nobody ever worked so hard or experienced such suffering in the history of the game. Cavalier middle-order batsmen might make snide remarks about bowlers being hired thugs who do nothing but stand at fine leg all day looking tired. But the reality is that bowling is, and always has been, the toughest part of cricket.

Pointing out that it takes twenty wickets to win a multi-day cricket match has become a favourite cliché in recent years, but what this means for the bowler is hours – and sometimes days – of toil, under the hot sun, or fighting a slippery ball and a headwind, knowing that his entire side (and sometimes his entire country) is waiting, with varying degrees of impatience or even desperation, for him to take a wicket.

And even if he changes the course of a game with a well-timed breakthrough, his lung-bursting efforts will almost certainly be overshadowed by a batsman. Brilliance by a batsman almost always represents a headline-grabbing century. Brilliance by a bowler might be two hours of miserly line and length for a return of 1 for 40 off 25 overs on a flat wicket against a pair of settled batsmen. Hardly the stuff of television highlights packages.

Bowling is a sporting vocation that takes great fitness, stamina and skill, but also great strength of character. It will never be as obviously glamorous or rewarding as batting. And yet nothing is more rewarding for the fast bowler than seeing the stumps fly or the batsman flinch, or, in the case of the spinner, seeing a batsman beaten in the flight and stumped yards out of his ground. Even the workhorse medium-pacer takes no less delight in seeing the ball nip or swing away, finding the edge, and carrying safely to the wicket-keeper, or jagging back to thump into the front pad plumb in front.

For millions, the quintessential cricket experience would be to watch Sachin Tendulkar or Brian Lara (or, in days gone by, Viv Richards or Sunil Gavaskar) stroke their way to a century with their characteristic blends of power and grace. But it is no less extraordinary or moving a sight to see a class bowler on song – an Allan Donald or Wasim Akram steaming in on those days when they are all but unplayable, when even the batsmen cannot help admiring their perfect combination of power, pace, accuracy and planning, as well as that extra touch of throttle that elite fast bowlers seem able to conjure up when the going gets tough. Similarly, being present to watch Abdul Qadir or Shane Warne or Muttiah Muralitharan dismantle a batting line-up, imploding the opposition's plans and dreams with pressure and guile, is an experience to relish.

No coach or teacher should ever make the mistake of nurturing batters at the expense of the bowlers. Encourage children to bat and bowl, and keep a sharp eye out for those who seem to especially enjoy bowling. Remember: batters are the 24-carat gold in your team, but a truly gifted bowler will be the jewel in the crown.

A BRIEF HISTORY OF BOWLING

The action of bowling is an unnatural and apparently illogical one. Why, an American observer might ask, doesn't the bowler simply throw the ball pitcher-style at the wicket in front of the batsman? Why deny himself the benefit of the huge leverage of a bent-arm throw, and deliver the ball at high pace without all that running in, over after over?

The answer to those questions lies in the history of the game, a history in which batsmen have, for various socio-economic reasons, always had the upper hand. Thus to understand the modern bowling action, it is important to investigate its history and evolution.

The *Oxford Dictionary of Cricket* suggests: 'It is arguable that the evolution of cricket has to a very large extent been determined by developments in bowling, rather than by developments in batting.' For several generations after the dawn of the game, the bowler simply rolled or tossed the ball along the ground, using an underarm delivery. The next change was the invention of the ball that bounced only once on its way to the batsman (what might be called a 'length' ball), and this dominated games of the mid-eighteenth century. It forced batsmen to fundamentally change their technique, and cricket became a game in which batsmen played forward and began defending, rather than standing back and swiping at the ball, much as hockey players do today.

But things really began to shift at the beginning of the nineteenth century, with the development of the round-arm delivery technique, in which the arm is held straight and more or less horizontal to the ground. Some enterprising historians have suggested that this change came about partly because women (who played the game recreationally) couldn't throw underarm while wearing wide skirts, hoops and crinolines. However, it is also likely that the effectiveness of the new style impressed bowlers. From about 1807 onwards, this kind of bowling was increasingly seen in official matches. Legislation lagged behind, but the round-arm delivery was finally given the imprimatur in 1835, with the stipulation that the bowler's hand could not rise higher than his or her shoulder. Of course by then, many bowlers had discovered that raising the arm above the level of the shoulder (with the wheeling effect that would look familiar to us today) made this form of delivery still more effective. In essence, round-arm bowling was a step en route to overarm bowling.

The crunch came in a notorious match in 1862, when Ned Willsher of Kent was repeatedly no-balled for bowling overarm by umpire James Lillywhite (ironically, the same Lillywhite who had previously been no-balled for bowling round-arm during his career as a bowler). It was a drastic action, but one calculated to force an institutional change. It took two years and much bureaucratic peevishness (a familiar situation for any follower of the modern game's politics) before the MCC finally voted to change the Law. The vote eventually went 27–20 in favour of the new technique, and the Law was changed in June 1864. The principal reason for the change, it was argued, was that bowlers were having problems taking wickets with the 'older' styles of delivery.

There have been other changes in the Laws of the game in the last 50 years that have had an impact (sometimes literally) on the bowler: for example, the reduction of deliveries per over from eight to six, no doubt a welcome relief to fast bowlers. But the most controversial change for bowlers in this time has been the no-ball Law, introduced in 1968, which is largely responsible for so many of the foot and back injuries currently ravaging the game at the highest levels. The reason is simple: since all bowlers have to cut the batting crease with their delivery stride, it means that they all land in and around the same place on the wicket as they get into their action. With three, four, or even five right-arm bowlers landing on the same square foot on the umpire's left, the landing area quickly becomes dented, then rutted, and finally concave. Bowlers must then either avoid this hole in the wicket, or must bite the bullet and land in it. Either way, they are forced to change the angle at which their foot is landing, thereby creating different forces in the body.

Prior to the introduction of this Law, bowlers could drag their back foot across the back crease, taking pressure off the front foot, as well as opening up a far greater landing area for their front foot.

This book discusses the standard of 'classic' bowling action, but if history has taught us anything, it is that what is standard today will be quaint and anachronistic in a hundred years time – if not much sooner. We might be presenting a current standard, but we are well aware that bowling actions are still evolving. Socio-economic circumstances are constantly changing, fewer and fewer children are getting access to physical education at school, and the lifestyles of most middle-class youngsters have never been more sedentary. The implications of these changes for bowling action are profound: as bodies become weaker and more prone to injury, actions will adapt and change accordingly.

New forms of the game are also influencing the old art of bowling. Limited-overs cricket has made accuracy – and the ability to bowl yorkers – essential, while even shorter versions, such as 20-over cricket, is bringing the medium-pacer to the fore, bowling on a length that is difficult to get under, and offering no pace for the batsman to use. But shorter, more frequent games and bigger winners' cheques also mean that bowlers are more tense, less likely to be bowling without having found a rhythm, and therefore putting substantially more stress on their bodies.

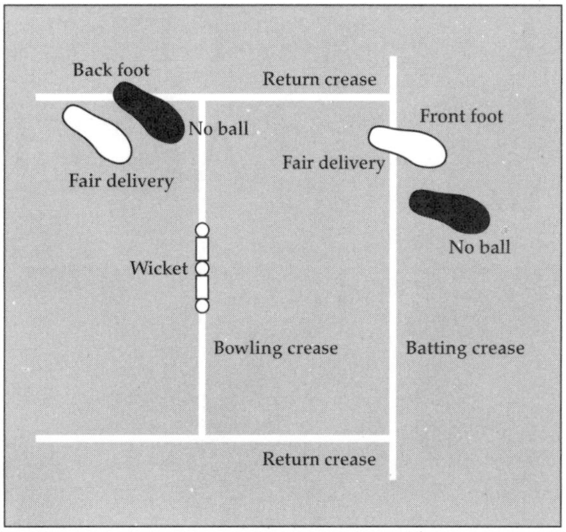

This is why this book begins with a discussion of the bowler's action, since this is the foundation upon which a bowler's skills are built. Too many coaches are lax in their approach to coaching bowling, perhaps a result of there being so many different methods in circulation. But most of these are based purely on trial and error, or personal experience, rather than on hard facts or research. There is a real need to establish baseline principles for teaching the basic bowling action.

So how does the basic action of bowling work? What is a sideways-on action? What is a mixed action? The answers to these questions are the first steps in fulfilling your bowling potential.

FIGURE 1: *The 'legal' position of the feet when bowling according to current Laws*

THE BASIC
ACTION

Whether you bowl quick outswingers or looping off-spinners, the basic aspects of the bowling action are the same. As the great English fast bowler John Snow (whom Bob Woolmer considered the best bowling coach in the world) points out, it is only the amount of effort put into the action, and the variation in wrist and finger movements, that define which type of bowler you are.

To describe this basic bowling action in words is rarely helpful, since it ends up sounding like a highly complicated manoeuvre and can discourage young players from ever trying it. To be fair, the five distinct movements that make up the bowling action are fairly complex, but when seen as parts of a smoothly executed whole, they all make sense.

The bowling action is built on three foundations: momentum, balance and timing. Momentum carries you to the point of delivery; balance allows you to be in control of your movements as you bowl the ball; and timing controls the finer nuances of the delivery, such as line, length and flight. To understand how important momentum and balance are in the bowling action, roll a coin along a table-top, and imagine that it represents a bowler, his arms and legs spread out to touch the edge of the coin. Any jerky or unco-ordinated movements, and the coin will begin to wobble, eventually losing momentum and teetering over onto its flat side. Bowling is no different: any interruption to the smooth cartwheeling action of the delivery, and the ball will go nowhere.

The bowling action, from the moment the bowler leaves his mark at the start of his run-up, until he jogs to a stop at the end of his follow-through, is a smooth and continuous effort; but for the sake of teaching, practice and analysis, we have broken it down into five distinct phases. These are:

1. The run-up and jump into the beginning of the gather
The front arm extends high (to the edge of the imaginary coin or cartwheel); the body turns sideways; the back foot is parallel to the crease; the head looks over the front shoulder; and the ball tucks in near the chin and points towards the target. John Snow says that at this point you are 'bringing your limbs, body and wits together like a boxer smoothly readying himself to throw a punch'. (Allan Donald had a famously 'low' gather, so in this picture the front arm is relatively low.)

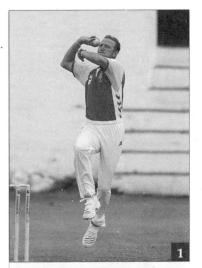

2. The set-up
The gather is completed. This is the start of the uncoiling spring effect: the front knee is brought upwards, so that the body rocks back; the bowling arm now begins to extend towards the bottom of the coin or wheel (see also side-on panel 3 on the opposite page – again, no two actions are identical).

3. The unfold
The bowler 'unwinds' towards the target; the front foot comes down and forward with the front arm (both arms are now virtually parallel to the ground); the head begins to follow the front arm down over the top of a braced and straightened front leg. Some 'give' in the front leg is acceptable to prevent injuries, as long as the front leg straightens out again at the moment of delivery. The bowler's eyes are fixed on his target.

4. The delivery

The head is level and the eyes in line with the chosen target; the bowling arm swings up and through the full extent of the coin, with the ball being released at the top of the arc, as the arm is about to swing down again. The bowling arm follows through fully towards the batsman, which is vital when getting the ball to swing, seam or spin: don't catapult the ball out of the fingers.

5. The follow-through

The body completes its 'circle' (with a turn of the hips) and the bowling arm follows the same path as the front arm. Allow momentum to drain away by running some way down the pitch if necessary: fast bowlers can actually injure themselves by stopping only three or four paces after their delivery. Snow explains that this stage is 'merely a relaxation and expending the energy of the delivery', which carries you off the wicket.

Many bowlers trying to bowl faster believe that they need to leap higher into their delivery stride, and push off to extraordinary heights. However, both bowlers and coaches should take note: it is height of the delivery that is important, not the leap. Keep your shoulder and arm as high, and your body as vertical, as possible throughout the delivery.

Another useful guideline – and a helpful coaching tool – is that of 'bowling downhill'. To get the effect of bowling with your weight going towards the target, and what it feels like to bowl over your braced front knee, imagine bowling down a slope or even a flight of steps. Perhaps even try this on nearby steps, going through your action as you rock from a higher step to a lower, and then onto the third step down with your follow-through. You should never feel as if you're running and bowling uphill.

SIDE-ON VERSUS FRONT-ON ACTION

The sequence discussed and illustrated above describes the classic 'side-on' bowling action, which is considered by many to be the ideal way to bowl: the body remains sideways-on to the target from the moment the back foot lands until the front foot hits the bowling crease; the bowler sizes up his target by looking over his front shoulder; and during the actual delivery there is a strong and sudden rotation of the hips, which generates power.

However, some bowlers prefer to have their chests facing the batsman during their jump and gather, and this is called a front-on action. Technically speaking a 'front-on delivery' is a misnomer, since all bowlers face the batsman chest-on at the moment they release the ball, but in the quick, smooth delivery action, the chest-on gather and jump look dramatically different to the side-on action.

Front-on actions are often regarded with considerable suspicion by coaches. Common criticisms are that this action restricts the bowler's ability to swing the ball away from the right-hander, and that the lesser degree of rotation in the hips means that there is less power behind the ball. Of course those who employ this second argument usually fail to recognize that the greater the turn of the hip, the more things can go wrong with the action, especially if there is not enough momentum in the bowler's run-up.

Certainly many of the most famous chest-on bowlers haven't been famous for their outswingers, and have tended to spear the ball into the pads. But when this group is headed by bowling legends like Malcolm Marshall and Wasim Akram, one should be very careful about dismissing it as an 'incorrect' action.

In fact, there is absolutely no reason why a coach should ever try to change a chest-on action to a side-on action if the chest-on action is working for the bowler and producing wicket-taking deliveries. Besides, research suggests that fundamentally changing an action that is already ingrained is almost impossible. The authors estimate that the most a coach can implement is a change of around 5% or less to a bowler's action – which is not so much a change as a tweak here and a fine-tune there. However, it will simplify matters when teaching bowling from scratch to ingrain a side-on action.

THE DANGERS OF A MIXED ACTION

While a front-on action may be considered unorthodox, there is nothing 'wrong' with it. A mixed action, however, can be downright dangerous, and all coaches should be on the lookout for it. A mixed action is one in which a bowler combines front-on and side-on postures in the same action, and this coaches *must* correct – ruthlessly if necessary – as soon as they see any hint of it.

When delivering the ball with a mixed action, the bowler lands his back foot (and therefore aligns his lower body) as if for a front-on delivery, the back foot pointing generally in the direction of the batsman. But he then twists his shoulders and upper body into a side-on position during the delivery stride. (The reverse can also happen.)

This high-speed contortion puts enormous strain on the lower back, which is being forced to rotate excessively, as the hips and shoulders are travelling in opposite directions; worse still, this strain is being exerted at the most vulnerable moment of extension – i.e., the point at which there is most strain on the spine. This leads almost invariably to injuries of the lower spine, including disc degeneration, bone bruises or even fractures. These can cut a promising bowler's career short, but yet more serious, can have crippling effects in the player's later life, years after he has ceased to play cricket. Many bowlers persevere with mixed action because it can be a very good way of generating pace and swing, but they do so at a cost: chronic injury almost always results from this action.

Coaches must know what a mixed action is, and then be able to spot and diagnose it. In this regard, video footage is helpful, but if you lack sophisticated equipment, the simplest way to check for mixed action is to ask the bowler to perform three normal deliveries in succession.

1. **During the first delivery, check the position of the feet and hips.**
2. **During the next, observe the position of the hips and shoulders.** (This should be enough to establish whether the two are in tandem or rotating in opposite directions.)
3. **The purpose of the third delivery is to ensure that you haven't missed anything, and confirm your diagnosis.** If you are in any doubt, consult an expert – preferably before the bowler has to pay a visit to an orthopaedic surgeon.

BOWLING OFF THE WRONG FOOT

Coaches may recommend this or that action, but a bowler adopts a particular action primarily because he finds that it suits him, is effective, and is comfortable enough to repeat for 30 overs a day. The result is not always a textbook side-on gather, delivery and follow-through, and one distinctive anomaly is the bowler who 'bowls off the wrong foot'.

The action is unmistakable: it looks awkward, based heavily on a strong, extremely fast rotation of the bowling arm, and a sort of flurrying hop rather than one powerful delivery stride and pivot. Mike Proctor was one of the most famous bowlers of this type. Batsmen found him more than a handful, as they had to deal not only with his express pace, but also his highly disconcerting action – the ball being released somehow later than they were expecting. This fact, that the ball was delivered fractionally after the front foot had touched down (so that the next stride was already beginning), gave the impression that the bowler was bowling off the wrong foot.

But as the sequence of Australian Max Walker below shows, this is an optical illusion. Walker lands on his back foot and transfers his weight onto his front foot as he bowls, just like most bowlers. There is a lovely high action, and a full follow-through. But where most bowlers plant their front foot and pivot over it, Walker –

and most of the other 'wrong-footed' bowlers – transfer much less weight onto the foot, instead touching down more on their toes than their flat foot.

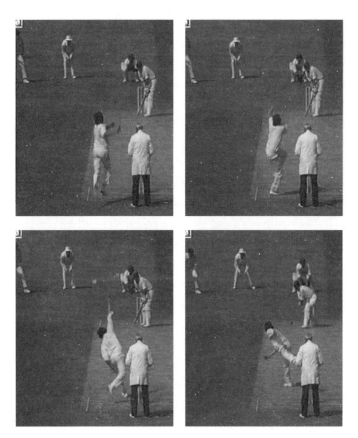

© Quintic

If the action is settled and grooved, and is producing good results for a young bowler, it should not be tampered with. In fact, the 'wrong-footed' bowler may even be sparing himself future injuries, since he spends much less time on his front foot, and is therefore not exposing his front knee and hip to repeated strain when he lands.

Sohail Tanvir, the young Pakistani medium-fast bowler, is the latest exponent of the 'wrong-footed' action. In his case, he combines his unorthodox delivery stride with the left-arm front-on action of probably the best left-arm fast bowler of all time, his countryman Wasim Akram. Hardly surprisingly, Tanvir is collecting a number of scalps at present. It remains to be seen whether opposing batsmen will learn to read him and respond appropriately.

THE RUN-UP

The nuances of the art of bowling have long been celebrated and coached, with pundits and commentators waxing lyrical about braced front knees, high actions, strong spinning fingers, beefy delivery strides, and so on. Yet in all of this close examination and discussion, strangely, the run-up has often been overlooked. Perhaps this has been because to those not versed in bowling, it seems a fairly simple and unglamorous activity: after all, why should bowlers be praised for running along in a straight line?

And yet every so often bowlers have come along whose talent and presence has forced even the most determined thrill-seeker to acknowledge that the run-up can be as dramatic as any fizzing leg-break or steepling short ball. Michael Holding, a medium-distance runner in his youth, became known as 'Whispering Death' as he cruised in smoothly and silently (umpires said they often couldn't hear him arriving at the crease), swaying as he ran, a sight many batsmen recalled as mesmerizing. Equally electrifying was Wes Hall, with a long-curving run-up, looking like a steam-train about to run over the batsman; and those who faced the uncomfortably fast Mike Proctor reported being thoroughly intimidated by his enormously long approach.

Not all bowlers indulge in distance and pace. John Price of Middlesex 'turned the corner', apparently running from mid-off towards the umpire, and then suddenly straightening. Derek Underwood would deliberately disappear behind the umpire before jumping out, almost ambushing the batsman. Bob Woolmer remembered facing Garry Sobers, 'so languid and easy in his run-up that it seemed impossible he would bowl at anything other than gentle medium pace, only to have the ball whistle past the bat.'

Were these great bowlers who happened to have great run-ups? Or were they great bowlers because they had great run-ups? The second question seems the more pertinent. In fact, it is not an exaggeration to say that the entire bowling action – and therefore the success of the bowler – is dependent on the run-up.

Yet many younger or inexperienced bowlers arrive at their run-ups through an almost arbitrary process, often marking out 'about fifteen longish strides' from a point more or less in the neighbourhood of where they're likely to be landing. At net practices, this haphazard approach becomes even more pronounced, with bowlers jogging in off wildly erratic approaches, alternating between energetic sprints of 20 metres and bored, lazy strolls of a few paces.

Still others are badly influenced by superstar role models. Having watched Shoaib Akhtar run in from 30 metres, young players can be lured into steaming in from a point well beyond their physical capabilities, arriving at the crease out of breath and in no condition to unwind into a good bowling action. Similarly, many aspiring spin bowlers have mistaken Shane Warne's apparently leisurely walk to the wicket for lethargy, not realizing that the Australian derived his power from his action and exceptionally strong forearms and fingers. So his fans mistakenly choose to take only two or three steps, instead of six or ten, or however many their particular action requires.

Perhaps they are simply being confused by the apparent contradiction of the run-up: it is vital to get it exactly right, to groove it perfectly until it becomes endlessly repeatable; and yet it is an entirely individual process. Inside about 20 metres, there is no 'ideal' run-up that a coach can enforce or train, and yet a great number of things can go wrong during this crucial phase of the bowler's task.

In other words, the run-up will always vary from bowler to bowler. Try to work out what feels right and comfortable for you. However, there are certain general guidelines that apply to all bowlers.

- Try to hit your mark at the beginning of your run-up accurately.
- Build your pace while running (or, if you are emulating Warne, walking) in – there is no need to sprint flat-out from the very first stride.
- You should hit your ideal running speed about three or four strides before the point of delivery.
- Your run-up must allow you to release the ball at maximum momentum, yet while you are still able to control the delivery.

The last point is crucial: bowling is largely about momentum, and this momentum comes entirely from your approach. Roll a coin along a flat surface, and watch how it begins to wobble once it loses its momentum: having travelled in a straight line (like a bowler delivering a ball with a grooved, balanced, side-on action) it now veers off either to the left or right – the equivalent of a bowler 'stalling' at the end of his run-up, and spraying the ball down either side of the wicket as he tries to force it through.

The sequences on the next page show a run-up that is more or less perfect: smooth, balanced on approach, gaining momentum from a strong, high leap and gather, which then allows the bowler to power through the crease beautifully.

WORKING OUT YOUR IDEAL RUN-UP

So what is the 'ideal' run-up? In a nutshell, it is whichever distance allows you to reach maximum momentum while still being in control of your movements.

Remember, just because your run-up is based on when you feel ready to bowl, don't assume that this feeling is a vague, variable undefined whim. Just as a long-jumper's approach needs to be measured out exactly, so too does a bowler's, both for purposes of momentum, and for the obvious reason that your front foot needs to cut the popping crease.

A note to coaches, however: if a young bowler is genuinely quick, don't be too hard on him if he bowls no-balls. Being overly strict about where his foot lands can often inhibit a young tearaway, and early in his career it is far more important that he learns to bowl quickly and accurately than to be concerned about whether he gives away a few extra runs in the form of no-balls. Later, of course, once he has learned the necessary control, he will need to be more disciplined!

WHEN, NOT WHERE

Bob Woolmer recalled: 'I was once observing West Indies seamer Vasbert Drakes, then just nearing the end of a superb career for Border in South Africa. Drakes seemed to be bowling too many no-balls for my liking, and I felt certain the veteran could bowl even better. I asked Drakes to demonstrate his run-up on a field, without stumps or any target at which to bowl, and told him to bowl as he would ideally like to – in other words, to deliver the ball at the precise moment he felt his momentum and control peak. I then watched to see if Drakes landed on the same place each time he delivered. In 90 minutes, the West Indian barely landed on the same spot twice. He had simply never worked his optimum running speed out in his own mind. Drakes was running in, seeing the white line of the crease approaching, and then putting in an extra stride before trying to get power behind the ball with his body rather than his momentum.'

The best way to calculate your optimum run-up is as follows:
- **Stand on the batting crease at the non-striker's end,** with your back to the wicket (i.e., facing in the direction of your run-up).
- **Push off and start running towards the outfield.** Start just behind the crease so that the same foot hits the crease every time you cross it. It doesn't matter which foot crosses the line, as long as you remember which one it is.
- **Run into the outfield, and bowl whenever your feel ready and comfortable –** you will feel when that is, almost as if a cork is working itself loose in you and getting ready to pop.
- **Ask a friend or teammate to mark the spot where your front foot lands when you bowl.** Repeat this process a few times to ensure that your rhythm is correct. This point now becomes your imaginary bowling crease at the end of your ideal run-up.
- **Walk back from that point to the popping crease, counting the number of ordinary steps it takes you to get there.** This is your optimum run-up.

RUN-UPS FOR FAST BOWLERS

Although there is no ideal length for a fast bowler, it seems that most fast bowlers run in from anywhere between 15 and 30 metres. Perhaps because the elite club of men who can bowl dangerously quickly is particularly macho, shorter run-ups have sometimes been frowned upon and derided as somehow inferior, but many bowlers have been deadly off 15 metres. Wasim Akram's approach was famously short, yet in his heyday he was one of the quickest bowlers in the world, and late in his career he

WOOLMER VS JUMBO JET AKHTAR

Run-ups hit the headlines in 2004 when Woolmer was quoted as wanting Shoaib Akhtar to shorten his run-up, while the Pakistani paceman in turn insisted he needed his long run-up, just as a jet aircraft needed a long runway to get airborne. The press made a meal of it, seeing a newsworthy conflict, but in reality Woolmer's suggestion had less to do with Akhtar's personality than technique and tactics. Under Woolmer's tutelage, Allan Donald had shortened his run-up because he felt he could bowl at the same pace off a shorter run for longer, which translated into longer spells. But Shoaib was taking around four and a half minutes to bowl an over, and Pakistan was getting fined for slow over-rates. Besides, anyone who runs in off 30 metres needs to be as fit as a triathlete to sustain it for 30 overs a day, and Akhtar's body was not always up to the demands he placed on it.

could still swing the ball both ways with superb rhythm. Richard Hadlee was another example of a fast bowler who continued to be as effective as ever off a shortened run, even if a journalist did complain that 'New Zealand's heaviest artillery was operating off a pop-gun run-up'. If a pop-gun run-up results in over 400 Test wickets, it can't be all bad.

Run-ups are measured in yards or metres, but it is as useful to think of them in terms of time: you might be releasing the ball at the spot you feel most comfortable, but you're also letting go at the *moment* you feel most comfortable. How bowlers push off into their run varies dramatically – some take lots of small steps very closely spaced, other begin by walking, others are sprinting by their third stride – and so it is difficult to find any kind of average duration. However, if we measure them from the point that the bowler hits his stride and settles into his rhythm, we find that the average length of a seamer's run-up is between 3,5 and 4 seconds. In other words, from the point he hits his stride and feels as if he's 'cruising in', to the moment of delivery, is 4 seconds or less.

When working with Allan Donald, Bob Woolmer found that the South African's ideal 'cruising time' was 2,74 seconds, after which he was at optimum pace to hit the crease: at 2,8 seconds, everything was ready to let go of the ball. Obviously players aren't able to count 2,8 seconds exactly while running in at full tilt, but Woolmer and Donald found that counting strides (with Donald's eyes shut so as to feel the optimum moment better without being distracted by the crease or other visual snags) got him as close to his ideal time as possible. In Donald's case, it was nine strides, and so he grooved his run-up and delivery accordingly: his delivery could be counted out as 9-jump-10-11.

Remember that just because you've found a length that suits you, don't be afraid to experiment with adaptations now and then during your career. Donald and Hadlee are examples of great fast bowlers who cut back their run-ups, often for less significant matches such as one-day games, purely to save wear and tear on their legs and backs, and then found that they were taking as many wickets – if not more – as before. Dennis Lillee even practised two run-ups: his standard long approach for full-tilt hostile pace, and another shorter one for those days when he knew his captain would need him for longer spells than usual.

RUN-UPS FOR SPINNERS

When Shane Warne dominated England in his first Ashes series in 1993, and then exposed catastrophic weaknesses in the techniques of South Africa's batsmen in 1994, he transfixed the sporting media. Much of the publicity he received focused on the extraordinary amount he turned the ball, the drift he got, his ear-studs and bleached hair, his sledging, and of course The Ball he bowled to Mike Gatting – a delivery that would set the tone for the next decade (we analyse it in depth on pp. 105–7).

In fact, in all the media attention and myth-making that always surrounded Warne, it is easy to forget that one of the aspects of his game that most startled and surprised pundits was his run-up. Batsmen and spectators alike were used to seeing spin bowlers jog in, or at least walk in quickly before breaking into a short jog just before they delivered. But Warne's slow walk, as menacing as any 30-metre run-up by a fast bowler, seemed quite new. This, allied to his phenomenal control and wicket-taking ability, completely revitalized the approach to a spinner's run-up.

Of course what Warne's run-up illustrates best is that, as with fast bowling, there is no ideal approach for the spinner. In fact, it could be argued that spinners present an even greater variety of run-ups that their quicker colleagues do. Warne's walk stands in sharp contrast to the run-ups of bowlers like Doug Wright, a superb wrist-spinner for England and Kent, who came in with a fast, bounding run off 14 metres, or Indian impresario Anil Kumble, who bobs and bounces his way to the crease. South Africa's Paul Adams had almost no run-up at all, getting into his action off no more than three or four steps.

In general, the spinner's run-up is worked out according to the same principles as those of the seamer: while momentum is naturally no longer an issue, the point of delivery must still come when the bowler feels most ready – balanced and rhythmical – to release; and the spinner's foot must likewise cut the crease. However, it differs in one major respect from that of a fast bowler: purchase.

The fast bowler's foot is the hinge of a lever or the anchor of a catapult. Some fast bowlers who seem to 'bowl off the wrong foot' (discussed on pp. 12–13) hardly even seem to need to plant their front foot. But most of a slow bowler's turn – the amount he spins the ball – comes from the purchase he gets with his front foot, as he turns on the ball of that foot during his delivery.

Slow down the big turner's delivery action, and you will see that his foot lands and then grips the pitch, only after which the twisting momentum of the body's action begins to drag it round. Some spinners try to bowl the ball as they land – often standing on the tip of their front foot – which results in very little spin, or none at all. This is a very common problem among young bowlers, and coaches need to notice when the hand is coming over in relation to when the foot is landing. If the front foot is down, planted, and ready to rasp round with the body's motion, he'll spin the ball. If he's landing as he bowls, he won't. South Africa's Claude Henderson was a prime example of this. Bob Woolmer noted, 'I first saw him as a promising 18-year-old who wasn't spinning the ball, and it was only after watching Henderson's feet rather than his arms and hand that I realized this was a general problem with spinners. I got him to bowl against his foot, rather than over it, and the result was impressive turn.'

Conventional manuals would no doubt cover this and related problems in a discussion on the bowling action, but many technical faults in spinners are directly linked to the run-up. For instance, left-arm spin bowlers have a destructive tendency to put their front foot over towards backward point or gully, which results in them trying to bowl around it. Suddenly, because of their unnecessarily angled arrival at the crease, it looks as if they're not spinning the ball at all. This is because they're spinning it onto a straight line, and the batsmen are hammering them to all parts of the ground.

In other words, it is the run-up that determines your position at the point of delivery, and the angles you are going to bowl. A good run-up and a good delivery position will mean getting more spin without changing your action.

RHYTHM AND SPEED

John Snow holds that the run-up has two phases. The first starts with an initial push or effort, translating into the first paces of your run, which gets you into a rhythmical running stride. The second phase sees you settle into your rhythm and gather the momentum that will drive you through your action. More importantly, the second phase of the run-up provides you with balance, which allows you to control and sustain all your movements throughout the gather and delivery.

This is a good analysis of the average run-up, but the issue of speed also needs to be addressed. Just as no two bowlers have identical run-ups, so no two people run at the same speed. How you approach the wicket and prepare for the gather is affected by many external factors: whether you're bowling uphill or downhill, how strong the wind is and what direction it's blowing, the length of the grass, the hardness (or bogginess!) of the ground, and so on. This is why you should always practise your run-up in the outfield before you bowl, to get your rhythm and to get a feel for the conditions.

The speed and rhythm of your run-up is also affected by your mental and emotional state. Perhaps it's your debut or a final, and you're excited with adrenaline flowing; or it might be your hundredth game and you're suffering from the 'Oh God, do I have to do this all again' syndrome. Maybe you bowled 30 overs yesterday, and your body is screaming for mercy.

In short, speed and rhythm are not only hugely variable from one bowler to the next, but can even change from day to day with the same bowler. However, in over 120 years of Test cricket, only the genuinely quick bowlers have run in very hard – men like Dennis Lillee, Allan Donald, Waqar Younis, Brett Lee and Malcolm Marshall. The rest have tended to cruise in off rhythmical smooth approaches.

A rhythmical run-up is one in which both feet start from the same places, and then repeatedly hit the same areas when running in. You'll have seen this in some Test matches, where a particularly long or angled approach begins to stand out from the others on the outfield by the fourth or fifth day, each footmark scuffed or worn, a sign that the bowler has been hitting the same marks over after over.

ADAPTING TO CONDITIONS

An optimum run-up is just that: it assumes that you're playing in ideal conditions, running in on a firm, level field on a fine day; but of course this isn't always the case. Conditions vary, and sometimes – particularly early and late in the season – they can be anything but perfect.

Being able to judge your run-up while taking conditions into account is therefore an important skill. Remember, your run-up itself shouldn't change: only change how you run. For example, if you're bowling into the wind, you're going to have to run harder, but not faster. If you're bowling with the wind, ease off a fraction.

You should also consider shortening the length of your run-up depending on the length of the grass and the hardness of the outfield. Grounds in Australia tend to be very soft, due to the sand-based soils used there for speedy drainage, so while your knees and ankles will be saved a pounding, your thighs will tire much more quickly than on a harder surface. Likewise, the grounds in Asia are rock-hard, providing plenty of spring in your step as you run in, but exerting much more strain on your joints.

Finally, bear in mind cricket's idiosyncratic conditions. Most southern hemisphere grounds are concrete bowls, engineered, built and planted from scratch, but in

England one can still find venues – even Test venues – that are simply expanses of village green that have been developed, complete with inclines in line with or across the pitch. In cases like these, take special care to practise your run-up thoroughly on the outfield to get a feel for its quirks.

THROWING

Any child old enough to throw a ball will have learned that the fastest, most accurate, and most economical way to propel the ball from here to there is to bend the arm back to the ear and then to straighten the elbow with some force, while transferring his or her weight forward with the throw. Baseball pitchers and fielders, who have pushed the art of throwing to its furthest extreme, get enormous speed and distance on their throws without taking more than a few steps, if that many. Indeed, every year dozens of pitchers in the professional leagues of the United States and Cuba send down fast balls as quick as anything bowled by just a handful of elite Test fast bowlers, without taking more than a single exaggerated step towards their target.

In light of this, and given the hundreds of kilometres that bowlers cover in a career of long run-ups, it would seem that bowling is both an unnatural and uneconomical action. But bowling is no more about speed and economy than batting is about hitting a ball a long way: baseball bats can propel a ball more than 100 metres into the bleachers, but if baseball's laws allowed for scoring behind the catcher, batters would find it almost impossible (or at least very dangerous) to try late-cutting or sweeping deliveries.

And it is here that the crucial difference between cricket and baseball arises. Baseball batters have two tasks: firstly they must prevent the ball from travelling through an invisible two-dimensional strike zone hovering a foot or two over home plate; and secondly, they must put bat to ball with only a very limited number of opportunities to do so, to get off base and get the scoreboard moving. These two tasks are inextricably linked: defence of the strike zone requires a stroke at the ball. They cannot opt to defend for three pitches and then attack.

Clearly theirs is not an easy task. But defending an imaginary target, even when having to play injudicious strokes in order to do so, is still considerably safer than having to defend a real one. A small strike zone means predictable lengths (all full tosses!), and generally predictable lines: in fact, the skill of batting in baseball lies largely in predicting or reacting to subtle, extremely rapid changes in line. A batter defending three stumps against a baseball pitcher would be in grave physical danger: no longer having to guide the ball through the strike zone, the pitcher could set about removing the batter in whichever (violent) way he saw fit, whether by breaking his toes with a yorker or by hurling a beamer directly at the body in the hope of sending him reeling back onto his stumps. Naturally even the threat of these injuries would be enough to get a batsman backing away and exposing his stumps, an easy target.

So thanks to the strike zone, baseball is an even contest between batter and pitcher. It is interesting to cricketers to see the outrage that often greets a pitcher hitting a batter on the body, either deliberately or by accident: entire teams pour out of the dugout and brawls are not uncommon. In cases of injury, lawsuits have even resulted. This would be unthinkable in cricket where blows to the body are not only common, but actively encouraged by aggressive captains and teammates. But the fury of baseballers in such cases stems from the equilibrium being broken, as an unfair advantage is claimed.

Cricket's batsmen are much more heavily padded than baseball's batters; and bowlers have long since worked out that the best way to hit the stumps or force an error is to bounce the ball rather than to bowl it on the full. Nonetheless, the dangers outlined above would still make bowlers the overwhelming favourites in cricket if throwing were the norm. A handicap is therefore necessary for bowlers. Instead of reducing the size of their target (and introducing penalties for missing the target as in baseball), cricket has adapted by reducing the bowler's speed. The result: a century-old ban on throwing, and the birth and flourishing of the peculiar straight-armed pitch we know as bowling.

Of course very few bowlers 'throw' deliberately: the universal condemnation of 'chucking', ingrained in every bowler since his or her first backyard game, makes it anathema. Besides which, unless throwing is regularly practised, it is extremely difficult to get right in the heat of battle without being noticed by the opposition and the umpire. Those who do throw the ball (perhaps trying to bowl an express bouncer) can expect to be no-balled. In this regard, club cricketers perhaps have an easier time of it than Test bowlers, as they don't face Code of Conduct violations, and feel free to launch lunchtime diatribes at offending bowlers, or to stop play to complain to the umpire.

However, no-balling Test bowlers has become increasingly fraught. The furore surrounding the controversial action of Muttiah Muralitharan has been protracted and heated (with the Sri Lankan even boycotting a tour of Australia for fear of being no-balled out of matches), while Pakistan's Shoaib Akhtar and Australia's Brett Lee have both been accused of throwing their faster bouncer. (We discuss Muralitharan's case and others like it in much more detail on pp. 34–7.) But these three cases pale in comparison with the treatment meted out to South African fast bowler Geoff Griffin, whose distinctly crooked elbow saw him no-balled out of Test cricket for good during a 1960 tour of England.

In cricket, a handicap is necessary to even out the contest between bowlers and batters – otherwise the former would have the advantage. Instead of reducing the size of their target (and introducing penalties for missing the target as in baseball), cricket has adapted by reducing the bowler's speed.

However proscribed and demonized, throwing persists in the modern game. It is becoming less common in first-class cricket, thanks to good coaching and rigorous policing, but nonetheless some bowlers continue to deliver the ball with a curious 'kink' in their arms, often appearing as nothing more than an especially flexible action or a subtle wobble in their forearm.

Here it is important to understand that throwing is not the result of a wicked bowler wishing to gain an unfair advantage. Instead, it is almost invariably the result of incorrect technique, and poor coaching. Coaches must be on the lookout for this wobble in young players so that it can be corrected before it becomes a problem: an adult action that includes a throw or 'chuck' will be almost impossible to correct.

Most at risk are young bowlers eager to bowl fast, but who don't yet have the strength, flexibility and co-ordination to do so. As they make the final effort, starting to 'heave' the ball down the wicket, the exertion will cause their trunk, shoulders and chest to turn and swivel both excessively and momentarily too soon, forcing the arm to bend and then release with a catapult effect. This is not only illegal, but also poses great risk to the bowler: the exaggerated arch of the back that results is likely to cause injury. If a young player persistently throws the ball, the coach should persuade him to try his hand at medium-pace or spin bowling instead.

THE GREAT CHUCKING DEBATE

Since the legalizing of round-arm bowling in 1830, cricket has struggled to define what constitutes a throw, or as it was originally termed, a 'jerk'; but the simmering debate came to a head in 1960, when the MCC ruled as follows:

> A ball shall be deemed to have been thrown if, in the opinion of either umpire, there has been a sudden straightening of the bowling arm, whether partial or complete, immediately prior to the delivery of the ball. Immediately prior to the delivery of the ball will be taken to mean at any time the arm has arisen above the level of the shoulder in the delivery swing. The bowler will not be debarred from the use of the wrist in delivering the ball.

The definition is clear and seemingly watertight: bowlers whose elbows are locked in full extension before 'the arm has arisen above the level of the shoulder in the delivery swing' are bowling legal deliveries. But things are not that straightforward. The Law on throwing, both in its original and amended forms (see opposite page), has a major flaw: it depends on what the umpire is able to see ('in the opinion of

All bowlers are now permitted to straighten their bowling arm up to 15°, which has been established as the furthest extension possible before becoming visible to the naked eye.

BUT DOES BOWLING WITH A BENT ELBOW REALLY HELP THE BOWLER?

Robert Marshall and Rene Ferdinands performed calculations at Waikato University, New Zealand, in an effort to address this question, providing and publishing scientific proof (in 2003) that bending and extending the arm during delivery does indeed increase the velocity of the delivery, largely through the increased internal rotation of the joints. Their calculations showed that the benefits of bowling with a bent arm are substantial: bowling with an arm flexed at 20° would increase the speed of the delivery by about 10km/h for slow bowlers, and by about 30km/h for fast bowlers.

either umpire'). Furthermore, the human eye is unable to spot a straightening of the elbow of less than about 10–15° during this phase of the delivery. In fact, it has now been shown that only extremely specialized scientific analysis can accurately identify a true 'chuck' – see the spread on pp. 28–33 for more details.

However, during the 1990s, increasingly sophisticated biomechanical analysis indicated that it was physiologically impossible to bowl with an entirely straight arm – a very small degree of flexion of the elbow was inevitable. The Laws were amended to allow the following: a bend of not more than 10° for fast bowlers, 7,5° for medium-pacers and 5° for spinners. But this too had to be abandoned after the Muralitharan controversy boiled over.

On 1 March 2005, the International Cricket Council (ICC) published its new guidelines on bowling actions, after a panel had analysed video footage of all the bowlers who had participated in the 2004 Champions Trophy. The panel steering the new guidelines featured former international cricketers, several of them bowlers such as Michael Holding, Angus Fraser and Tim May. It was widely assumed in the media that this pedigree would encourage acceptance of the new rules in the cricketing world. In the words of Sunil Gavaskar, the change to the Laws was 'a cricketing decision, proposed by cricketers for cricketers'. Cynics and critics took a different view, suggesting that it was a cricketing decision proposed by businessmen for the benefit of just one cricketer, Muttiah Muralitharan (a claim we examine more closely later).

The new regulations included an overhaul of the processes that had been used to identify and deal with suspect actions, and also focused for the first time on throwing at junior levels. However, at its heart was a dramatic new change in the Law: all bowlers would now be permitted to straighten their bowling arm up to 15°, which had been established as the furthest extension possible before becoming visible to the naked eye.

This was a remarkable departure from past recommendations, which had suggested that fast bowlers be allowed to straighten their elbows up to 10°, fast-medium bowlers up to 7,5°, and spinners up to 5°. The sudden 10-degree bonus for spinners further raised the suspicion of those who believed the entire development had been for the benefit of the Sri Lankan off-spinner – and, to a lesser extent, Indian off-spinner Harbhajan Singh.

The politics can be disputed, but what is beyond doubt is that any degree of extension of the arm will provide an advantage to the bowler. The changes to the Law, publicized as a firm measure to solidify and control the issue of throwing (a kind of legal firebreak, giving ground in order to stop further advances), may well have the effect of promoting throwing. Allow a bowler to flex up to 15°, and he will try his utmost to flex at 15° in order to gain the advantages that extra flexion provides. The changes to the Law may also lead to dramatic changes in the bowling action of spinners – from side-on to front on.

Marc Portus, a senior research scientist employed by the Australian Cricket Board and a specialist in fast bowling, has developed a system by filming bowlers in actual cricket matches, from which he is able to produce an image of the bowlers' skeletons (see panel below). By filming ten international fast bowlers and two first-class players from five different nations, he was able to calculate the extent to which their elbows extended (straightened or 'jerked') as their arms progressed from the horizontal (frame 1) to the vertical (frame 4) immediately after ball release. Bear in mind that the Laws (which initially stated that the elbow should not extend during this period of the

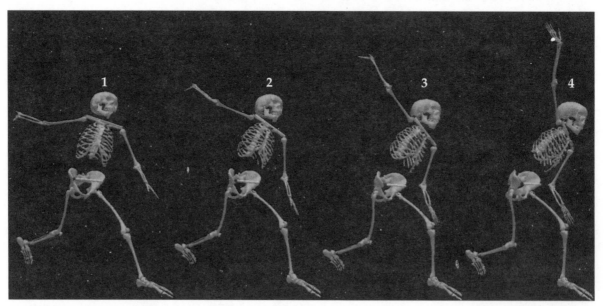

SOURCE: MARC PORTUS, 2003, AUSTRALIAN CRICKET BOARD

delivery) were amended to allow an elbow extension of 10°. But Portus found that of the 34 deliveries from the 21 bowlers he analyzed, 13 (38%) exceeded the 10° limit set by the ICC (see Figure 2 below). Interestingly, the majority of these bowlers were considered to have impeccable bowling actions when judged by the naked eye. Clearly, the naked eye is unable to see a great deal of 'jerking' in some of the world's best bowlers.

On the basis of his findings, which he presented at the Second World Congress of Science and Medicine in Cricket, Portus proposed that the ICC should consider extending their tolerance threshold to 16° (as shown in Figure 2). With this tolerance level, only 6 of the 36 deliveries (14%) would have been classified as illegal. The ICC subsequently increased the tolerance level to 15° (Portus et al., 2003).

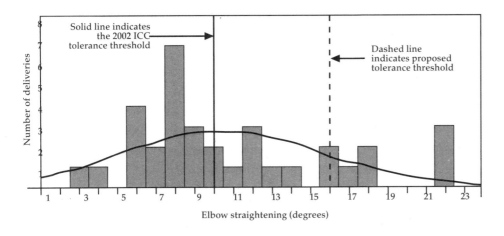

FIGURE 2: *Differing tolerance thresholds for elbow extension by fast bowlers, showing the proportion of deliveries considered illegal according to different tolerance thresholds*

Another problem with the MCC's original 1960 definition – indeed, with the entire debate currently agitating the sport – is that it focuses only on the result, and not the cause, of the throwing action. Throwing begins in the lower body and the trunk, with the upper arm only responsible for completing the action. Thus a true definition of throwing must include analysis of the action of the lower body and trunk. This assertion has revolutionary implications for the game, in particular coaches and administrators. However, as often happens when the game of cricket faces change, there is a tendency to cling to tradition, and many have yet to get to grips with the implications of Portus's findings.

SEEING THINGS: THE 'CARRYING ANGLE' – OR WHY THROWING CAN'T BE DETECTED BY ON-FIELD UMPIRES OR CAMERAS

The calling of Muttiah Muralitharan and certain other bowlers for 'throwing' in recent years presented the ICC with a challenge: it was now necessary to *prove* that these bowlers did actually 'throw' according to the current regulations. The ICC thus commissioned a series of biomechanics laboratories around the world to undertake such testing.

Among this group was a testing centre at the University of Cape Town/ Medical Research Council Research Unit for Exercise Science and Sports Medicine at the Sports Science Institute of South Africa in Cape Town, South Africa.

In the process of testing a number of bowlers with suspect actions, Kerith Aginsky, a PhD student in cricket biomechanics, noted that all had a similar fixed anatomical abnormality, known medically as a large 'carrying angle'. This is commonly found in women, but is less common in men. This abnormality causes the lower arm (below the elbow) to deviate from a line drawn down the centre of the upper arm. This can clearly be seen in the photo below of a bowler standing with his arms fully extended to his sides. In his case, the deviation is 17° from the vertical, so his 'carrying angle' would thus be 17°.

Aginsky wondered whether this carrying angle might contribute to the

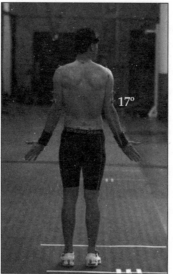

illusion of a thrown delivery in a bowler who was in fact bowling legally – in that he was not extending his elbow by more than 15° during the bowling action. She noted that Muralitharan also has a large carrying angle, and that he had reportedly been able to bowl effectively even with a brace on his elbow which prevented excessive elbow extension. This further suggested that Muralitharan's action, proven scientifically to be legal, might appear to be illegal because of an optical illusion, and that the latter might be influenced by the presence of his large carrying angle.

SOURCE: AGINSKY ET AL., 2008

To test this hypothesis, Aginsky and Tim Noakes used the opportunity provided by working with South African spinner, Johan Botha, who was being investigated for a suspect bowling action (Aginsky et al., 2008). Botha, like Muralitharan, has a large carrying angle. By using high-speed cameras and sophisticated biomechanical analyses, it was possible to establish that Botha's action (which, after much remedial work is now legal, as he extends his elbow by less than the cut-off value of 15° for both his off-spin and doosra deliveries) nevertheless gives the illusion of a throw, especially when viewed either on the field by an umpire standing at one spot for the entire delivery action, or when viewed in two dimensions from a single camera position. It was also established that the essential problem is that the bowling action occurs in three planes, whereas video footage in particular represents movement as if it occurs only in two planes. This explains why the illusion of a throw can occur in the action of bowlers like Muralitharan or Botha, both of whom have large carrying angles.

Scientifically, the 'throwing' movement of interest to the ICC is the extension of the elbow by more than 15° during the bowling action. The movement of flexion/extension occurs in the plane best seen when the elbow is viewed directly from the side, so that bony protrusions (epicondyles) at either side of the elbow joint point directly at the viewer or the camera (see below).

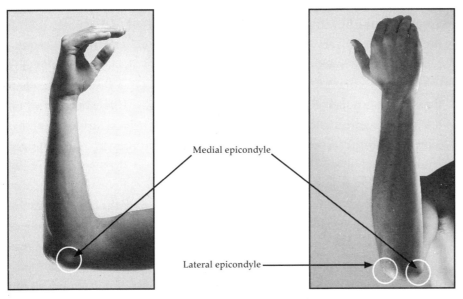

Medial epicondyle

Lateral epicondyle

View of the elbow showing the medial and lateral epicondyles, either of which must be at 90° to the viewer if throwing is to be detected with the eye or camera.

In contrast, when the elbow joint is viewed directly either from the front or from behind, the exact degree of elbow/flexion cannot be determined (because this movement is occurring in the plane at 90° to the viewing plane). However, any abnormal angle that is seen will relate to the carrying angle, since this angle can only be properly viewed from directly in front of or behind the elbow (at 90° to the epicondyles).

The important lesson from this explanation is that whenever one views the elbow in order to detect 'throwing', one must first check which view of the elbow one is seeing. If one is viewing the elbow from either directly in front or behind, the angle that is seen is the carrying angle. Only if the elbow is viewed directly from the side, can one be absolutely certain that one is viewing the movement of elbow flexion/extension.

What this means is that for an umpire to be able to identify a 'thrown' (illegal) delivery, he must be able to observe the elbow in such a way that he views only the movement of flexion/extension throughout the bowler's delivery action. This means that throughout the bowling action, he must be positioned at exactly 90° to the side of the elbow so that either of the elbow epicondyles points directly at him. This in turn means that if he (or a camera recording the bowling action) stays in the same place, then the elbow must remain in the same plane (at 90° to the viewing position) for the entire duration of the bowling action. If the elbow rotates out of that plane during the bowler's delivery action, then what the umpire sees (or the camera records) will no longer be solely the result of elbow flexion/extension. It is exactly these circumstances that favour the illusion of a throw, even when the elbow has not extended during the bowling action. This is because when the bowler's arm is at the horizontal position in the delivery stride, the elbow joint is pointing directly upwards, so that a viewer positioned exactly at right angles to the batting crease will see only the flexion/extension angle of the elbow (see Figure 3 opposite).

However, when the bowler's elbow goes beyond the vertical at the moment of ball release, the elbow has rotated by about 90°. As a result, at the moment of delivery, the epicondyles of the elbow no longer point across the pitch in a line parallel to the batting crease. Instead, they now point down the length of the pitch. As a result, the only position from which the flexion/extension angle of the elbow can be observed at the point of delivery is either directly behind or in front of the bowler.

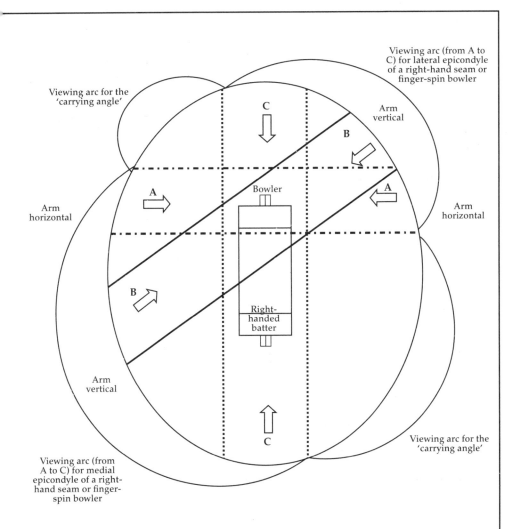

A: Directions from which elbow flexion/extension can be detected when arm is horizontal during the delivery action (position 1 in panel on page 226).

B: Directions from which elbow flexion/extension can be detected when the arm is vertical before releasing the ball (position 4 in panel on page 226).

C: Directions from which elbow flexion/extension can be detected at the moment of ball release.

FIGURE 3: *Viewing arcs for detecting throwing at different moments in the bowler's delivery action*

SOURCE: AGINSKY ET AL., 2008

It follows that the extent to which the elbow extends during a bowling delivery can be determined only by comparing the angle of flexion/extension when the arm is horizontal (by viewing the elbow from the mid-off or mid-on positions – A in Figure 3) and at the moment of ball release (by viewing the elbow from a position directly in front of or behind the bowler – C in Figure 3). Since no human umpire can be in both positions within the approximately 100 milliseconds that it takes for the arm to move that distance, no human umpire is ever in a position to call a bowler for throwing during the actual course of play. The only way for a human umpire (or a camera) to stay at exactly 90° to the elbow joint (so that any elbow extension during the bowling action can be detected), would be for him to be transported in an arc from mid-off to behind the wicket-keeper as the bowler's arm comes forward in the delivery stride. Similarly, a camera (or set of cameras) used to detect 'throwing' would also have to travel through that arc in about 100 milliseconds.

Given that neither of these techniques is available during matches at present, our proposal (Aginsky et al., 2008) is that bowlers with apparently questionable actions should no longer be 'called' during the course of play, given that it is not possible to detect a thrown delivery simply by observing with the naked eye. Instead, the bowler should be referred for expert biomechanical analysis at an ICC-accredited laboratory. If such testing shows that the extent of elbow extension does indeed exceed the ICC criteria, only then should the bowler's status as a 'chucker' be made public and remedial action begun. There is no doubt that real damage has been done (sometimes unjustly) to bowlers' careers in the past by umpires and referees insistent that their action fell beyond the bounds of legality.

What is it about the actions of Muralitharan and Botha that makes it seem 'obvious' that they are 'throwing' to those who view video clips of their bowling actions? The answer is that it is an illusion caused by their large carrying angles when viewed in two dimensions from a single vantage point, typically from a camera positioned either directly in front of or behind the bowler's arm.

If we consider the view from directly in front of either of these bowlers, we would first see the right hand appear above the horizontal, followed by the elbow. But at this stage, the front of the elbow is pointing directly towards the viewer. Thus any angulation that is apparent to the viewer cannot be due to elbow flexion/extension, since this cannot be seen from the front of the elbow (as already explained). Thus any angulation that is seen can only be the result of the carrying angle. However, if the bowler has a large carrying angle (as do Muralitharan and Botha), the viewer will have the impression that the elbow is bent as it comes forward.

However, as the elbow approaches the vertical, the upper arm begins to rotate through 90° so that at the point of release, the elbow is seen from its side, that is, with one of the epicondyles pointing directly towards the viewer. In this position, the angle that is observed is the flexion/extension angle; the carrying angle is not seen in this view and has consequently 'disappeared'.

So, because the upper arm rotates as it moves forward during the bowling action, a viewer from either in front or behind the bowler will first see the carrying angle appear and then suddenly disappear as the arm reaches the horizontal. This will give the unwary viewer the impression that the elbow has straightened, causing a 'throw' or 'chuck'. In this way, the illusion of a throw is created in those bowlers with large carrying angles like Muralitharan and Botha, even when they do not extend their elbow more than the legal amount permitted by ICC rules.

Finally, there is one additional factor complicating the detection of the 'thrown' delivery, especially by the modern generation of spin bowlers. Data shows that spin bowlers like Muralitharan and Botha not only extend their arms during their bowling actions; as their arm moves forward from the horizontal towards the vertical, the elbow initially flexes (bends backwards) before beginning to extend (bend forward) rapidly, as each bowler 'flicks' the elbow to impart maximum spin to the delivery.

This means that an umpire wishing to detect a throw by a modern spin bowler would have to detect when the elbow reaches its maximum degree of flexion (sometimes before the arm reaches the vertical position), compute that angle, and then subtract that angle from the elbow angle at ball release. If the final number exceeds 15°, then the ball has been 'thrown'.

Obviously, no human would be able to detect with certainty this range of movement, happening as it does in such a short time, even if they were somehow able to be in exactly the right positions at both moments (maximum degree of elbow flexion and ball release). Only sophisticated biomechanical analysis is able to perform the necessary calculations.

THE SPECIAL CASE OF MUTTIAH MURALITHARAN

When the Sri Lankan match-winner was first no-balled for throwing, during the Boxing Day Test in Melbourne in 1995, his supporters were quick to allege home-team bias on the part of umpire Darrell Hair – no stranger to controversial decisions. The Australians were threatened by the emergence of a world-class spinner to rival Shane Warne, they insisted, and had reacted accordingly. But when Hair called Muralitharan again in one-day games in Brisbane and Adelaide in 1999, calling his action 'diabolical', the accusations became even more charged, with racial bias being alleged.

For a decade, Sri Lanka's cricketing pride has been largely built around Muralitharan. Chaminda Vaas was a tireless presence with the new ball in Test and one-day matches, and Sanath Jayasuriya had electrified the game in the 1996 World Cup, but it was Test victories that mattered, and the spinner stood alone as their match-winner, often single-handedly bowling his team to victory with endless spells as his colleagues rotated at the other end. An accusation of what boiled down to cheating against their champion bowler was an attack on the national pride of an entire country. Sri Lankans were livid.

However, more objective commentators were not convinced that Hair had acted in error. Bishen Bedi, the great Indian spinner of the 1970s, who had one of the cleanest, most classic actions in the game's history, didn't pull any punches when he wrote, 'If Muralitharan doesn't chuck, then show me how to bowl. He looks like a good javelin thrower.' In August 2007, Bedi confirmed that he was gunning for Muralitharan's reputation when he declared that the Sri Lankan would probably reach 1 000 wickets in Tests, but that those wickets 'would count as mere run-outs' in his eyes.

But the accusations of racist bias looked increasingly troubling as first Pakistan's Shahid Afridi was accused of throwing his fast leg-break, and then Indian Harbhajan Singh's doosra raised eyebrows. Australian umpires and purists remained as rigid as ever, refusing to countenance a slackening of the Laws regarding the straightening of the arm (despite coming under pressure from critics to investigate the action of their own Brett Lee – like Shoaib Ahktar, accused of throwing his fast effort ball). By 2003, their dogmatism was widely regarded in the Asian cricket world as stemming from a mixture of insecurity and racism, the former apparently fuelled by an historic series win for India against Australia the same year, the scintillating final Test as loaded with nationalist pride as it was with sparkling cricket.

By 2004, the atmosphere of suspicion between white and Asian cricketing administrations had intensified. It did not help that of the sixteen bowlers reported by umpires standing in international matches for a suspect (throwing) action in the preceding decade, the vast majority were from Asian Test-playing countries. Only one player each was referred from Australia, England and South Africa. Meanwhile, the ICC's move to Dubai, a strategic shift away from London and Sydney, and the

'If Muralitharan doesn't chuck, then show me how to bowl. He looks like a good javelin thrower.'

– Bishen Bedi

apparently insatiable appetite for one-day cricket in Asia, were all fertile soil for conspiracy theorists who believed that Asian cricket's financial clout, nationalism and an ever-hungry Asian television audience would see the Laws on chucking bulldozed to suit the politics of the day. The March 2005 change – which essentially legalized Muralitharan's action – came as no surprise to them.

However, those more deeply involved with the Sri Lankan's case found answers less easy to come by. The first complicating piece of the puzzle appeared when Muralitharan's action was investigated at the University of Western Australia and the Hong Kong University of Science and Technology, and the results were published in the scientific literature in 2000. The findings (Lloyd et al., 2000) revealed that Muralitharan has a congenital abnormality of his elbow, making him unable to extend his elbow fully. In medical terms, he has a fixed flexion deformity of his elbow of 37°, which means that he is unable to bend his elbow through the final 37° to the fully straightened position. The implications of this were intriguing: the spinner was, it seemed, literally unable to straighten his arm, and was therefore physically incapable of chucking. In addition, Muralitharan has a large 'carrying angle' (see photograph on p. 28), which makes it look as if he throws regardless of whether of not he actually extends his elbow during his bowling action, described in detail below.

Which is not to say that he doesn't flex his elbow at all during his delivery. Sophisticated biomechanical observation and analysis show that the spinner's elbow angles 180 milliseconds before ball release (arm aligned vertically downwards); 107 milliseconds before ball release (arm horizontal); and at ball release for each of his three deliveries: off-spin (Figure 4a), top-spin (Figure 4b) and leg-spin (Figure 4c).

Muralitharan is literally unable to straighten his arm, and is therefore physically incapable of chucking.

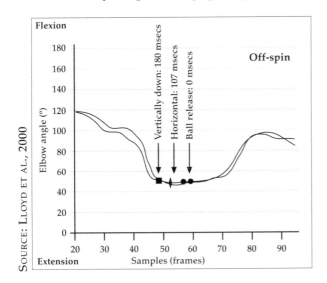

FIGURE 4A: *Degree of flexion when Muralitharan bowls off-spin*

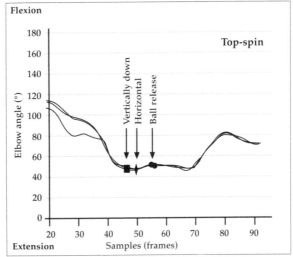

FIGURE 4B: *Degree of flexion when Muralitharan bowls top-spin*

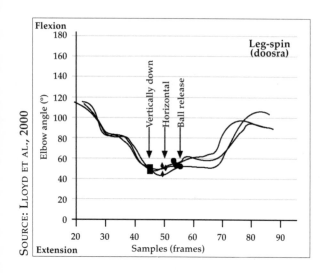

SOURCE: LLOYD ET AL., 2000

FIGURE 4C: *Degree of flexion when Muralitharan bowls leg-spin*

These results show that virtually all the extension in Muralitharan's elbow occurs before his arm enters the final 180 milliseconds of his delivery action, as his arm passes from pointing vertically downwards, through the horizontal and vertically upwards to the point of ball release; that he bowls with his elbow bent at about 45–50° of flexion; and that his elbow hardly extends at all during the final 180 milliseconds of his delivery action. Furthermore, in that arc of the delivery movement, his elbow actually flexes 3,5° when bowling the off-spin and top-spin deliveries, and 7,9° when bowling the leg-spin delivery. Note, however, that this action is opposite to the one used in defining a throw. Thus, since a throw is conventionally defined as an *extension* (straightening) of the elbow during this phase of the delivery, Muralitharan clearly does not throw if this definition is followed. According to the study's authors, 'the elbow is essentially at full extension from when the upper arm is aligned horizontally until ball release, and no extension of the elbow occurs during this epoch; therefore, he does not throw' (Lloyd et al., 2000, p. 980).

However, in purely scientific terms, this conclusion is not entirely correct since Muralitharan does not bowl with his elbow 'essentially in full extension'. Rather, he keeps his elbow flexed by about 13° from its 'essentially fully flexed position' and then he bends (flexes) it a further 3–8° as he bowls.

Whether you consider Muralitharan's action an illegal aberration or a legitimate technique that will give slow bowlers a fighting chance in a game increasingly stacked against them, the fact remains clear that modern spinners have redefined the way the ball is released and spun. Also beyond dispute is that these spinners are seen as role models and icons by a generation of young cricketers. There are literally thousands of young Muralitharans and Harbhajans bending their elbows and bowling leg-breaks with an off-spin action throughout the Asian subcontinent and elsewhere. Indeed, during the Under-19 World Cup in 2004, no fewer than six spinners were sent home for remedial work on their actions.

Purists and the anti-Muralitharan lobby might insist that this was an admirable piece of police work – that these players and their coaches needed to have certain rudimentary facts of cricketing life explained to them. But in the opinion of Bob Woolmer and his co-authors, the action taken against them was a last act of desperation by the old cricketing order, trying to turn back the rising tide. What we are seeing is not a degeneration of coaching, but rather an evolution in bowling, similar to that of the mid-1880s, when underarm bowling gave way to round-arm bowling.

If you don't like it, don't blame coaches or Asian cricket, and certainly don't blame Muralitharan. If you want to blame something, look no further than covered pitches, helmets, heavy bats, shortened boundary ropes and smaller grounds. Cricket is simply shaking itself back into some sort of equilibrium, and for the first time in almost 30 years, finger-spinners are back in the game.

RHYTHM AND ACCURACY

As mentioned earlier, John Snow believes that rhythm is the bedrock on which all bowling is built: rhythm gives you balance, which gives you control, which allows you to get yourself into the right position to bowl.

It is not surprising, then, that when a bowler finds himself struggling on one of those days when nothing seems to be coming together, he is likely to tell his captain that he 'can't find his rhythm'. Whether slow or quick, bowlers need a rhythm as much as batsmen do, perhaps even more so, since a batsman can get through a lean patch by scratching odd singles or leaving the ball. A hopelessly 'out of synch' bowler, however, is likely to be hit out of the park and then dropped from the attack.

Bowling rhythm is an overwhelming sense of everything working as it should, a feeling that the body, ball and bowling crease together make up a well-oiled machine that simply needs to be turned on and let loose.

GETTING YOUR GROOVE BACK

But all good things must come to an end, and all bowlers lose their rhythms at one time or another. This can happen for a variety of reasons. The bowler might be stiff or unfit, or bothered about some aspect of his action, or worried about a niggle that might presage a full-blown injury. Perhaps some family matter is weighing on his mind, or he thinks he is being over-bowled and feels resentful, or he is simply jaded after playing too much cricket for too long.

Some bowlers spend longer in the nets, breaking down their actions with their coach, or watching video footage of themselves; those who aren't professionals can afford to leave the game for a week or two to try and 'detox'.

But some of the great bowlers developed their own unique methods for recovering or maintaining their rhythm. Richard Hadlee would ask a fielder he trusted (or the wicket-keeper) to watch him for any obvious causes. In the meantime, he'd ask his captain to take him off briefly and then bring him back on (the equivalent of getting back into bed so that one can get out again on the right foot). Dennis Lillee would jog

Rhythm is what gives you balance, which gives you control, which allows you to get yourself into the right position to bowl.

'Forget what your

arms, legs, shoulders

and body should be

doing. If your rhythm

is right, they will look

after themselves.'

– Peter Philpott

up and down the field, visualizing himself as a steam engine building up power; and Australian wrist-spinner Peter Philpott would envisage his rhythm, trying to hear it and feel it, and then 'count' himself back into it.

The important point is not to go on trying to force your rhythm to return: Lillee and Philpott's colourful methods also point to the importance of visualizing the ideal performance state. The irresistible mental picture of hard man Lillee trotting up and down the outfield, possibly muttering 'I think I can, I think I can', is testimony that even the most macho player can benefit from visualization.

Indeed, Philpott's thoughts on rhythm are vital, and bear repeating:

Forget what your arms, legs, shoulders and body should be doing. If your rhythm is right, they will look after themselves. For this reason, it is a worthwhile exercise at practice – but only when you are bowling well – to 'listen' to your approach, visualize your run-up, and 'hear', 'feel' and 'see' the rhythm of your bowling. Awareness of your own personal rhythm when you are bowling well becomes valuable when you are not. Rather than worrying about where your arms and feet are… concentrate only on your rhythm. Get it back to what it should be… and it all comes back together.

Captains should recognize that they can play a vital part in getting their bowlers into a good rhythm: if your strike bowler is struggling, the answer may be as simple as taking him off and bringing him on again later, as Hadlee sometimes requested. Consult with him, and call on him once the pitch, overhead conditions, wind direction and end are more to his liking. We've all seen bowlers who were taken to the cleaners during their first spell come back and almost immediately take a break-through wicket. Often, this is simply a matter of finding their rhythm. If the captain stays supportive and relaxed, this should not become an entrenched problem.

RHYTHM AND ACCURACY: WHICH COMES FIRST?

Accuracy is conditioned by the position of the bowler's head. If his rhythm is right and his head is in the right position, the ball will go where he wants it to: the head needs to travel horizontally along a plane as he bowls, and when the player's rhythm isn't working, the head can fall away or remain too upright.

Some coaches encounter young spin bowlers who can turn the ball a long way, but who aren't accurate. They assume the child has to make a choice between spin and accuracy until he works out his action and develops his own rhythm. But once again, this is a failure to understand that accuracy comes from the head: whether you bowl looping leg-breaks or fast outswingers, if your head travels smoothly along the horizontal, you'll land the ball where you want it to go.

Bob Woolmer had a simple way of demonstrating this: 'When I want to make bowlers (especially young leg-spinners) aware of what their heads are doing – and therefore what is happening to their accuracy – I ask them to head-butt my hand. I put my hand out, fingers up and palm towards him (rather like a policeman telling the traffic to stop) and ask the player to bowl at me without the ball. However, I insist that he hits my hand with his forehead. The results are usually remarkable: bowlers can aim with their arms and shoulders and hands, but get them to hit a target with their heads, and they go to pieces! Most fall away to the off side, or they're too high and go down the leg side.'

Remember, the stillness and the position of the head is crucial to becoming a successful bowler.

PRACTISING FOR ACCURACY

A theory gathering momentum is that modern bowlers do not practise enough, a notion perhaps given weight by the lack of accuracy of many bowlers currently playing at all levels of the game.

This waywardness has many causes, such as poor actions made worse by too much one-day cricket – adventurous and aggressive batsmen force modern bowlers to be reactive rather than pro-active – but bowlers must also accept some of the blame. Incorrect head-positions and defective run-ups are all very well, but if you are not practising accuracy, you have no chance of becoming accurate.

To this end, we recommend target bowling, one of the most old-fashioned practice methods in the game, but one that is still highly effective. Start with a rectangular mat (car foot mats are ideal) placed 6 to 8 feet from the batting crease, and one stump to aim at. Gradually reduce the size of the mat, and begin to move it around once your aim starts improving. This way you can practise good length balls, deliveries that are short of a length, bouncers, yorkers, and so on. Repeat this drill for an hour a day (punctuated by two breaks for stretching and replacing fluids) and you should be on your way to being able to land the ball exactly where you want to – or in cricketing parlance, 'having it on a string' in the way a fly-fisherman has his fly on a string and can drop it on any spot he wishes.

Whether you bowl looping leg-breaks or fast outswingers, if your head travels smoothly along the horizontal, you'll land the ball where you want it to go.

LINE AND LENGTH

The bowling action is the sequence of movements that allows the bowler to get the ball up the pitch towards the batsman; but simply bowling the ball in the batsman's general direction is not good enough. In fact of all the major ball sports, perhaps only baseball and basketball require a thrower to hit a smaller target; but in neither of these sports is the thrower who misses his target as severely punished as cricket punishes the wayward bowler. The pitcher who sends a curve-ball into the batter's shins is not likely to be picked up and slammed for a home run into deep left field; and the basketballer who misses a free throw can be fairly certain that the defence under the basket is not going to catch the missed shot and sling it a full court-length for a three-point basket.

In other words, as soon as the action is mastered, it is time for the bowler to shift his sights up the pitch towards the batsman. A good action will make this range-finding adjustment far more easy and natural, but all bowlers must nonetheless understand line and length and practise them until they are second nature if they are to succeed.

But why talk about line and length at all? Surely, if the bowler's task is to send the stumps flying, he should simply focus on landing the ball on the correct length in line with the stumps? Well, yes – if there weren't a batsman between him and stumps, a player trained since he could hold a bat to defend and deflect and clobber! Knocking over the stumps is the glorious ideal of all bowlers, especially the quick men, but they need to remember that there is more than one way to dislodge a batter. Castling a batsman is a rush, but it is just as rewarding to see him tripping over his front foot, plumb LBW, or fishing outside off-stump to nick an outswinger or a leg-break to the keeper or slips, or hopelessly stumped. Each of these dismissals needs to be conceived, plotted and executed. And the key element in their execution is aim – or line and length.

Lines and lengths for bowlers vary according to a number of factors. For instance, a good length on a hard, fast wicket might be considerably shorter than a good length on a soft, damp one. Similarly, a tight line for a leg-spinner bowling to a right-hander is completely different to a tight line for a right-arm fast bowler prying at a left-hander's weakness outside off-stump.

Figure 5 shows a very impressive grouping of deliveries to a left-handed batsman, all pitching on a good length, and all in the discomfort zone outside off-stump. But clearly this pattern would be catastrophic for a leg-spinner, to either a left-hander or a right-hander: a good length for a fast bowler, with the ball coming through quickly and confusing the batsman as to whether to play forward or back, suddenly becomes a juicy long hop from the spinner, giving the batsman all the time in the world to cart him through mid-wicket or square leg.

Similarly, one shouldn't assume that this is a graphic revealing an experienced bowler like Glenn McGrath working over a left-hander: it could as easily reflect the unhappy results of a frustrated fast bowler trying to blast out a right-hander by bowling around the wicket into his body, but not dropping it short enough, and being picked off pads and thigh-pad for easy singles.

In other words, line and length depend on the pace of the bowler, the pitch, the strengths or weaknesses of the various batters, the type of bowler, and even the weather. Finding the attacking line and length that perfectly suits the circumstances is the real skill of a bowler, and one of cricket's more engrossing challenges.

LENGTH

So all coaches, whether they know what they mean or not, will urge their bowlers to settle on a 'good line and length'. But what do these two terms actually mean?

The length of a delivery is determined by how far up the wicket the ball lands. Since a wicket is 22 yards long, it would seem that there are literally hundreds of possible lengths to bowl, from a yorker landing on the base of middle stump, to the embarrassment of dragging the ball down with the arm and releasing it straight at the bowler's own foot. In reality, only the batsman's half of the pitch contains the range of lengths bowlers should use, since anything shorter can only result in a long hop, or a perhaps a bouncer that balloons safely over the batsman's head. Which of these lengths you use as a bowler depends on your own personal preference and conditioning, and the specific tactics you are employing at the time.

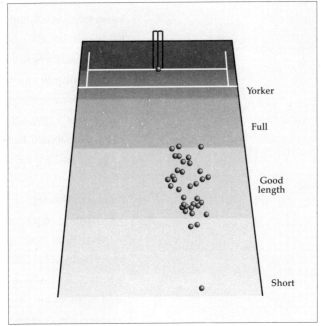

ADAPTED FROM HAWKEYE DATA

FIGURE 5: *Good-length deliveries from Glenn McGrath to a left-handed batsman. Note the exceptional control of line as well as length – nothing to drive, cut or pull.*

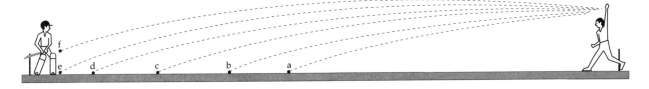

a: Long hop
b: Bouncer (short ball)
c: Good length
d: Half-volley
e: Yorker
f: Full toss

FIGURE 6: *Different length deliveries as bowled by a medium-fast bowler*

Long hop: Sometimes called a half-tracker, this pitches very short, only about halfway down the pitch or perhaps even closer to the bowler's end. It is a delivery that will have your coach and captain tearing their hair out, since it gives the batter plenty of time to pick his shot and smash the ball to the boundary. Cut this ball out of your game completely, unless you are a genuinely quick bowler, in which case (on a good wicket) your long hop is likely to be a bouncer. Even so, fast men like Brett Lee and Allan Donald have found themselves bowling long hops on particularly slow wickets – and paying the price.

Bouncer: Although this delivery pitches on more or less the same length as a long hop, it differs in pace and bounce. Whereas the long hop dawdles invitingly through to the batter at hip-height, the bouncer shoots up off the pitch towards the batsman's upper body or head at tremendous speed, forcing him to evade the ball or fend it off. It is the least subtle and most brutal of the fast bowler's weapons, and is generally used to intimidate. The rules of cricket were changed in 1991 to limit the number of bouncers that could be bowled per over (a move fiercely contested by the West Indies and Pakistan, respectively the undisputed winners and runners-up in the Great Bouncer Wars of the 70s and 80s – a period in cricket history when short-pitched pace bowling, as opposed to spin, swing and seam, became the tactic of choice against batsmen). Today the bouncer tends to be used sparingly to surprise or unsettle the batsman, often before the bowler follows up with a fuller-length delivery.

The West Indian bowlers of the Bouncer Wars era, known as 'ear, nose and throat specialists' by their hapless opponents, not only perfected intimidation, but also concocted a vocabulary that illustrated the pleasure they took in their frightening work. For example, a particularly lethal bouncer was a 'perfume ball', so-called because it gave the batsman a sniff of leather as it hurtled up past his nose. A ball that reared and spat at speed off the wicket was said to have 'done a cobra' on the batsman. And for batsmen desperately looking to get forward and score a few runs? 'If you want to drive, go rent a car.'

Short of a length: This is a ball that pitches closer to the batsman than a bouncer or long-hop, but not close enough to be ideal. Nevertheless, although this can also give the batsman the opportunity to score, it does not give him as much time for shot selection. This means that it can sometimes be effective in preventing the batter from scoring. On an uneven or very bouncy pitch, it can even result in a wicket, as it can rush the batsman into a hasty shot, which gets caught.

Good length: For seamers or faster bowlers, this is a ball that pitches about four metres from the batsman's crease (although of course the exact spot will depend on the condition of the pitch: the slower the pitch, the further up towards the batsman that spot will be). A ball on a good length presents two problems for the batsman:

- he now has less time to decide which shot to play (as there is less time to watch the ball after it pitches);
- he is uncertain about whether to play off the front or back foot. The object of a good-length delivery is thus to create doubt in the batsman's mind.

Half-volley: Usually the half-volley is nothing more than four runs, neatly gift-wrapped and presented to the batsman. On a good wicket, it allows him to drive as the ball pitches, removing the threat of lateral movement, as well as presenting him with a ball bouncing almost exactly into the middle of his bat's sweet spot. However, because batsmen's eyes light up when they see a half-volley, it can make them overconfident, so that they rashly chase wide or swinging half-volleys, resulting in an edge to the keeper or slips. Pitching up the odd half-volley is therefore not a bad tactic. However, you don't want to be bowling them over after over and hoping for edges: that way lies ruined bowling figures and lost matches.

Yorker: A deadly length, especially when bowled at speed. Also called the 'toe-crusher', it usually takes the batsman by surprise, which makes it very difficult to 'dig out'. Because of this element of surprise, and the fact that it reaches the batsman barely a centimetre off the ground, taller batsmen (such as tail-enders) can be particularly vulnerable to it, since it takes them fractionally longer to get down to deal with it. The only reason we don't see more of this great wicket-taking delivery is because it is difficult to get its length exactly right; bowlers striving for yorker-length deliveries often bowl a full toss instead.

Full toss: Another gift-wrapped boundary for the batsman, but this time without any of the risks that accompany reaching for a wide half-volley. The ball does not pitch on the wicket at all, and is effectively a free hit. A full toss from a spinner should – and often does – go for six. However, not all full tosses are necessarily train-wrecks: a low full toss (one that arrives around ankle-height) can be a difficult delivery to get underneath in the final overs of a one-day game. Still, this is a delivery to be avoided.

Beamer: One of the few acts on a cricket field that can get players genuinely angry in an instant. The beamer is a full toss bowled between hip and head height, usually at pace. It is extremely dangerous, since batsmen rarely pick it up (having expected a ball to travel

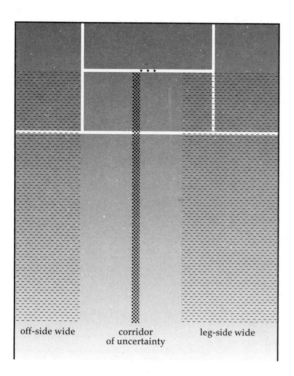

off-side wide   corridor   leg-side wide
of uncertainty

FIGURE 5.7: *Conventional lines for bowling to a right-handed batter (reverse for a left-hander)*

It is a cardinal sin for a bowler to bowl a line that benefits the batter in any way.

down towards the pitch), and it can cause fatal cardiac arrest if it hits the chest, or equally fatal injuries to an unprotected head. The beamer is unsporting and has no place in the game of cricket.

LINE

Line deals with the direction in which the bowler delivers the ball, and is determined by the target he is aiming for. As with length, this target might vary according to the circumstances and rules of the game, but it will never stray too far from the bowler's primary prey: the batsman and his wickets.

The see-saw battle between bat and ball has never been more clearly illustrated than in Figure 5 on p. 41; showing Glenn McGrath bowling on a good line and length to a left-hander, it demonstrates that in cricket, the difference between success and failure is measured in centimetres. Get a ball over the top edge of a flashing cut shot wide of the off-stump, and you've won a moral victory. Get it past the toe of a bat playing the identical shot, and the umpire is likely to call your delivery a wide. You'll be frustrated and the batter will be understandably smug.

As mentioned, you are free to bowl whichever line you feel will produce the best results, but whatever you choose, remember this: it is a cardinal sin for a bowler to bowl a line that benefits the batsman in any way.

Whether this means bowling down the leg side to a player who is strong off his pads, or bowling leg side when your captain has given you an off-side field, you cannot afford to give the batsman an inch. After all, he's not pulling any punches when he hits you to the fence. Also remember that an overly defensive line (which you might believe is frustrating the batsman into playing a rash shot) could be doing nothing more than allowing him to get settled, get his eye in, and costing you a wide or two per over.

This last aspect of your line – accuracy – is a crucial one, especially in the modern limited-overs game. Umpires have become extremely unforgiving, especially concerning deliveries going down the leg side – most international bowlers will know the frustration of being called wide for sending a ball over the top of leg stump. Master your line, and you master your own bowling destiny.

It is worth remembering that changing your line is as effective a weapon as any in your arsenal. For some reason younger and less experienced bowlers find it far easier to vary their length than their line, but the two are equally effective, and combined, these variations can be a real handful for batsmen.

Figures 8a and b illustrate how line and length are often used as individual weapons by a pair of bowlers working in tandem. England's Marcus Trescothick was on the receiving end in this case. Peppered by Brett Lee, whose explosive lengths and express pace would have posed problems but at least opened up scoring opportunities, he was also confronted by Glenn McGrath's almost robotic control of line, every ball but the two on the extreme left and right pitching in the danger zone just outside off-stump and on a good, nagging length. In this case, both bowlers exerted pressure in different ways, providing a perfect foil for one another. This combination of pace and precision is an ideal partnership, one that has been extremely successful for such pairs as Donald and Pollock, Waqar and Wasim, Ambrose and Walsh, and even McGrath and Warne.

TAKING AIM

Knowing where you want to bowl the ball as you run in is one thing, but where do you actually aim as you get into your delivery stride?

Most great bowlers say that they look at a spot on the pitch as they unwind into their delivery, although some report simply having a feel for the line and length they're going to bowl, and end up delivering 'blind'. This is largely a matter of personal taste. Bob Woolmer read that Brian Statham looked at the base of off-stump, and duly copied Statham. When Statham wanted to bowl a yorker, he just raised his sights so that he was looking at the top of off-stump. Other bowlers aim for areas on the pitch. Fred Trueman would choose a spot when he wanted to bowl a bouncer, and then try to hit that spot. He wasn't worried about the end-result: by hitting that spot he knew what line the ball would take. He left the ensuing mayhem for the batsman to deal with! Terry Alderman went through a phase when he was almost unplayable bowling to left-handers. He claimed to be aiming at the wicket-keeper's left hand, which would make it very difficult for the batsman to find his off-stump.

One-day cricket has also introduced new challenges for the bowler, as batsmen move around in the crease as the ball is delivered. However, a good rule is to aim to hit the top of off-stump: if you coach young bowlers, drum this into their heads and good results will follow. Naturally, the length for hitting the top of off-stump will vary according to the pitch, but you can't go too badly wrong using this guideline.

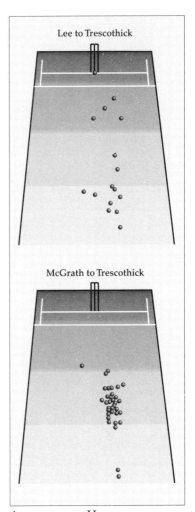

ADAPTED FROM HAWKEYE DATA

FIGURE 8A AND B:
Australia works over England's Marcus Trescothick – bombarded by Lee, nagged by McGrath.

MEDIUM-PACE AND FAST BOWLING

Perhaps because they have the same action and bowl the ball seam-up, medium-pace and fast bowlers are invariably lumped together, whether in cricket manuals like this one or by coaches organizing a net session. But the reality is that the two types of bowler are entirely different breeds, each demanding a specific set of physical, emotional and intellectual skills.

Of course, these differences haven't gone unnoticed by opinion-shaping pundits over the decades, with each generation imposing their own cultural norms on each type of bowler. For instance in the late 1890s, anyone bowling genuinely fast would have been seen as something of a ruffian, a working-class brute with more brawn than brain. By the 1950s, fast bowlers were being accorded more respect, but class distinctions were clear: bowling fast was exciting, but not nearly as skilful – or refined – as bowling medium-fast swing and seam. Frank Tyson may have been greased lightning, but it was Alec Bedser who was knighted.

But class distinctions weren't the only factor influencing public debate. Racial stereotypes also came to the fore in the 1960s as the first great West Indian quick bowlers began to appear. Wesley Hall's pace and aggression thrilled English and Australian spectators, but to many – even mainstream media commentators – his ferocity was a reflection of his blackness. The Big Bad Black Bowler had emerged, a stereotypical image that still persists. Even the most painstakingly politically correct commentators imply that there is nothing quite like watching a tall black fast bowler steaming in, whether Michael Holding, Curtly Ambrose, Devon Malcolm or Makhaya Ntini – the implication always being that black fast bowlers are 'in their natural element'.

Of course the famous pace quartets of the West Indies in the 1970s and 1980s did nothing to dispel this impression, even sometimes actively engaging with it as the Caribbean team embraced Black Power and Black Consciousness, giving their cricketing style the faintest of ideological edges. But the stereotypes remained, and many survive intact in the modern game: racialized fantasies that require great spinners to be Indian, histrionic swing bowlers to be Pakistani, dashing batsmen to be Australian, and so on. It is one of cricket's great ironies that modern adults, who would be appalled and embarrassed by assertions that Italians are excitable, Arabs duplicitous and Orientals cruel, suddenly start talking about 'natural rhythm' the moment a West Indian or black South African bowler sets foot on a field!

But the public perceptions of the fast bowler and the seamer have never remained constant for long. By the 1980s – largely thanks to the talented and disciplined heroics of the West Indian pacemen, as well as Dennis Lillee, John Snow, and Imran Khan – the idea of the 'thoroughbred' fast bowler had been established, suddenly imbuing quick bowlers with the class they had always been denied. But at the same time, the elegant and cunning swingers and seamers found themselves demoted in the public eye. In the press and commentary box, they were now referred to as 'trundlers', 'workhorses' or even 'pie-chuckers'. Pace had become king, and swing and seam were admired only when they happened at speed, as performed by Ian Botham or, later, Waqar Younis.

The purpose of this chapter is to give both medium-pace and fast bowlers their due. Current social trends and tastes might make fast bowling more glamorous than the bowling done by less speedy players, but it shouldn't be forgotten that the vast majority of wickets taken every day on thousands of cricket fields around the world are claimed by medium-pacers, just getting the ball to do a little bit. Also remember that a great many world-class quicks mellow in their later careers into medium-pacers of great skill.

So what does it take to bowl the ball seam up, and to bowl it well? The attributes of the genuine fast bowler will be discussed shortly, but they do overlap somewhat with those of the 'workhorse' seamer or swing bowler.

The most essential qualities of the good medium-fast bowler are:

- **Stamina:** Andrew Flintoff (at the faster end of medium-fast) bowled 14 overs on the trot at the Oval in the 2005 Ashes series, a titanic effort for a big man running in hard.
- **Strong stomach, chest and shoulders:** the stronger your stomach muscles, the more resilience your back will have to cope with the huge stresses that bowling seam-up puts on it.
- **Aggression:** this doesn't necessarily have to take the form of physical threat. A medium-pacer pitching up five consecutive swinging half-volleys is showing as much aggressive intent as the fieriest fast bowler trying to knock off a batsman's head. You must want to take wickets.
- **Height:** interestingly, this is truer of seam bowlers than genuine quicks, since those who rely on hitting the seam need to be tall and strong in order to bang

By the 1980s, pace had become king, and swing and seam were admired only when they happened at speed, as performed by Ian Botham or, later, Waqar Younis.

the ball into the pitch and get purchase.

- **Patience:** perhaps the greatest attribute of any bowler, slow or quick.

Combine these qualities in a fit, focused and skilled young bowler, and you will produce a more than handy medium or fast-medium bowler. But making a fast bowler is a different matter altogether…

CREATING A MONSTER: THE FAST BOWLER

While there is no denying that bowling fast is one of cricket's most physically demanding tasks, the champion fast bowler is more than the sum of his parts. The great English bowler Fred Trueman summed this up when he said, 'There has never been a successful fast bowler who didn't have fire in his belly… you must be a fast bowler in heart, mind and body.'

But to be a fast bowler in heart and mind, you first need the body. Bob Willis said in order to be genuinely quick, the bowler must have 'the ability to whip his arm over quickly at the time he delivers the ball… unless that ball leaves your hand quickly, you'll never make a fast bowler.' All are agreed that real speed is one of the fundamental assets all quickies need. So how fast is fast?

While a 'fast' delivery is usually clocked at around 140km/h or above, most fast bowlers operate in the speed zone between 130 and 155km/h. Most of the top fast bowlers of the last few decades have all clocked up about the same pace, with one or two able to bowl an exceptionally quick delivery; but to the batsman facing the barrage, the difference between 145km/h and 155km/h is more or less irrelevant, especially if the bowler has got the line and length right.

Arm speed is vital, but the one common trait of all great fast bowlers over the decades is best expressed by the great Wes Hall: 'Man, if you want to be fast, you gotta be loose.'

Suppleness is key to speed, and certainly all the great fast bowlers we've studied, from Trueman to Allan Donald, have been extremely 'loose': in his prime, Donald could sit with his legs straight in front of him and knees locked, and reach 23 centimetres beyond his toes. Michael Holding was all but fluid, and even a muscular 'effort' bowler like Jeff Thomson was extraordinarily lithe. Recalling Thomson's elasticity, Alan Knott said that 'for a big man, he was like a piece of rubber'.

The second asset of the dangerous fast bowler is height. Of course, cricket has a long and splendid history of quick men who were below average height (Malcolm Marshall leads a field that includes Harold Larwood, Ray Lindwall, and Darren Gough), but standing at 6 foot or more will always give the fast bowler an advantage.

'Man, if you want to be fast, you gotta be loose.'

– Wes Hall

The shorter men can get the ball to lift dangerously off a length with the best of them, but the tall bowler will always worry the batsman because of the trajectory of his delivery and the steepling bounce. On more rustic or dilapidated grounds, where the presence of sightscreens has become haphazard, facing a tall fast bowler can be a nightmare, especially if the ball is coming down out of dark trees or an overcast sky.

Height not only presents a physical threat, but the steeply bouncing ball can also be extremely difficult to score off. Some of the greatest bowlers in the game's history have stood well over 6ft 4, men such as Curtly Ambrose, Courtney Walsh, Joel Garner and Glenn McGrath, and it is no coincidence that this elite group also boasts exceptional economy rates, proving almost impossible to score off when they were on song.

The third trait fast bowlers share is athleticism. It may seem an obvious asset, but at lower levels of the game, speed of bowling and athleticism can be confused, as young undeveloped bowlers wreck themselves bowling as fast as they can, while genuinely gifted athletes go unnoticed, bowling spin or medium-pace, or sometimes not bowling at all. A good basic guide for coaches of very young players is a simple foot race: whoever crosses the finishing line first has the potential to be a fast bowler. A rough calculation by a journalist some years ago suggested that during the 1997/98 season, South Africa's opening pair of Allan Donald and Shaun Pollock covered a distance equivalent to three marathons, just in their run-ups!

Strength goes hand in hand with athleticism, and, like the fast-medium bowler, the quick man needs excellent upper body strength and a strong trunk (stomach, hips, hamstring and buttocks), not only to bang the ball down into the pitch 90 times a day, but also to protect him against injuries. Batsmen risk injury from the balls they face, but the fast bowler's injuries arise purely from what he does. No other player is as vulnerable to injury, or as negatively affected by it. A batsman can keep going with the odd niggle or two, but even a minor strain can render a fast bowler ineffective, or remove him from the game altogether.

Fourth in the fast bowler's armoury is his weight: he can't afford to carry any excess fat. This doesn't mean that overweight (or even fat) bowlers can't send the ball whistling around the batsman's ears (almost all batsmen have been worked over at some stage by a chubby steam-engine of a bowler, sweating and blowing as he gets the ball to hum through to the wicket-keeper); but if a fast bowler is to be successful at the top level of the game for any period of time, he needs to shed as much fat (but not muscle) as he can. While not all bowlers should starve themselves in the hopes of looking like Glenn McGrath (dubbed 'the one-iron with ears' by his teammates), it is a fact that any excess weight puts further stress on the body and front leg during the delivery stride.

A rough calculation some years ago suggested that during the 1997/98 season, South Africa's opening pair of Allan Donald and Shaun Pollock covered a distance equivalent to three marathons, just in their run-ups!

The fifth attribute of the fast bowler is youth. While spinners tend to improve as they mature, fast bowlers have a limited shelf life. Richard Hadlee, Imran Khan and Courtney Walsh extended their careers well into their late 30s; McGrath's age-defying performances continued until his retirement from Test cricket at 36; and Wasim Akram maintained a lively pace well into his 'autumn years', taking his 500th ODI wicket at the age of 37. But just a handful of men out of hundreds suggests that early mid-life is not a place that takes kindly to fast bowlers.

Indeed, most of these bowlers don't qualify as genuinely fast: Hadlee and Khan geared down their pace as they grew older, relying increasingly on guile and swing, Wasim's run-up shortened with each passing year, and McGrath was never express to start with. Exceptional fitness, rigorous stretching and a sensible run-up will prolong the fast bowler's career, but he must accept that the clock is ticking once he turns 30, and if he's still letting the ball fly with venom and fire at 33, he's doing very well indeed.

The final trait of the thoroughbred fast bowler – the willingness to work – is perhaps the most important of all, and is best left to one of the greatest of that elite breed to explain:

Nothing in life comes easy, and fast bowling is no exception. To reach the top and remain there you must be prepared for blood, sweat and tears. Blood in your boots after bowling your heart out on rock-hard wickets, sweat in bucketsful left on the training track, and tears of frustration when things aren't going right for you.

To be a good fast bowler you must be prepared for the sacrifices, to make the extra effort in everything you do, to listen and learn at all times, to take the good with the bad, and above all other things to believe in yourself and your ability to bowl out the best batsmen.

There is no easy way to the top, believe me, and that's the way it should be. Those who reach the top and think that the hard work is all over soon find how wrong they are. It's simply a case of work, work, work, and then more work.

(Dennis Lillee, 1982, p. 17)

To sum up, the six vital attributes of the fast bowler are:
- **suppleness**
- **height**
- **athleticism/fitness**
- **low body fat**
- **youth**
- **above all, a fantastic work ethic and huge determination.**

THE DELIVERIES

The action provides momentum. It powers the ball down to the other end, and sends it along the line and (to a lesser extent) the length the bowler wants it to go. But it is the wrist and hand that dictate the subtler, more dangerous, variations of the delivery. With a rhythmical run-up and a clean action, you've installed the rocket-propulsion system in the missile; now it's time to attach the warhead.

Variation is nothing without control, and before you begin experimenting with various weapons in the medium- and fast-bowler's arsenal, you must be comfortable with the standard grip employed by all seam-up bowlers.

The first two fingers rest on either side of the seam (or on the seam, if you prefer), with the side of the thumb on the middle of the seam beneath the ball, and the fourth and fifth fingers providing balance. The ball should rest on the last joint of the fingers, with a small gap in between it and the cupped palm of the hand. This space is very important – if you grip the ball too tightly, or wedge it too deep in your fingers, it will leave your hand too slowly, and you are also likely to lose a great deal of control over it.

Gripping the ball too tightly also has negative physiological consequences: it locks your wrist and elbow, and generally tenses the body. This saps speed, flexibility and co-ordination at the moment you need them most – when delivering the ball. A locked wrist also means you'll struggle to seam or cut the ball (discussed further in the pages that follow).

So how does the seam-up bowler take wickets? How does he go from being cannon-fodder, putting the ball on the pitch for the batsman to do as he pleases with it, to being a dangerous, probing, intelligent bowler?

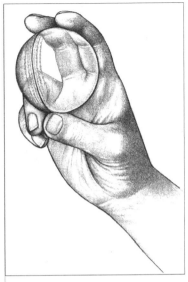

Standard grip for fast and medium-pace bowling

BABY BOWLERS

Those coaching beginners might like to investigate the special cricket balls that have finger-markings that show youngsters the correct places to grip the ball. These are useful aids to those learning both pace and spin bowling.

Do not, under any circumstances, try to teach young boys or girls how to bowl using full-size 156 gram cricket balls in the hope that they will get a 'head start' or 'grow into them': their hands are too small, their fingers too weak, and it will not only wreck their technique, but cause frustration that could turn them against the game for good.

A fast or medium-pace bowler takes wickets in four ways:

* **with seam**
* **with swing**
* **with pace**
* **with his brain.**

The last weapon depends on a good grasp of the first three. Even out-and-out pace can have its limits of usefulness. Besides, only a tiny proportion of seam-up bowlers playing at any time have the rare combination of physical and technical talents that enable them to be genuinely quick.

The vast majority are medium or medium-fast bowlers, plying their grand old trade with the tried and trusted weapons passed down through generations by the dynasty of seam and swing. From Alec Bedser and Keith Miller to Terry Alderman, from Imran Khan to Shaun Pollock and Glenn McGrath, the more subtle – and intelligent – art of moving the ball off the pitch or through the air is a vital one to master. And like so much else in cricket, it takes hours of painstaking work to add this to your armoury.

1. SEAM

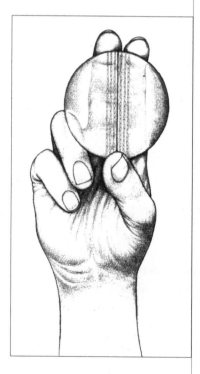

Grip for seam bowling

The seam bowler relies on one of cricket's more ironic quirks: predictable randomness. While the swing bowler or the spinner knows where he wants the ball to end up, the seamer doesn't. In fact he doesn't have the slightest idea where the ball will go after pitching. But neither does the batsman; and when a good seamer is hitting his straps on a helpful pitch, he can be as much as a handful (if not more so) than a tearaway paceman bowling fast away-swingers.

The principle of seam is simple: land a round ball on a proud, angled seam, and it's as good as landing it on an unevenly shaped stone in the pitch. On the right line and length – where the batsman is drawn forward and has little time in which to adjust – the slightest deviation can take the edge or nip back through the gap between bat and pad.

The grip

The grip for bowling seam is almost identical to the standard fast/medium-pace grip. However, there is one important distinction. While the standard grip allows for minor variations in the angle of the seam, seam bowlers need to release the ball with a perfectly vertical seam, and with the wrist held straight behind the ball, to give the seam the greatest chance of landing on the pitch.

The action

The classic seaming ball is delivered with a very high bowling arm, and a loose wrist that flicks down the seam behind the ball. This 'back-spin' creates stability in the ball's flight and prevents it from wobbling off the vertical, and also allows the seam to grip the wicket when it pitches.

Height is crucial to getting the ball to hit the seam and deviate. Shorter bowlers need to focus on getting their arm up as high as possible, but the ideal seamer is a big, strong man. This is because in order to get the seam to bite and bounce, you need to hit the deck hard. Try to make contact with the ground as hard as possible. Skidding the ball through will not work: the seam will skim the pitch, instead of gripping and jagging away at an unpredictable angle.

Glenn McGrath and Courtney Walsh are two good examples of how important height is to the seamer: the ball comes down from seven or even eight feet in the air, and is banged in short of a length. Walsh in particular had an uncanny ability to land the ball on the seam, even though his deliveries often seemed to be wobbling around dramatically during their flight.

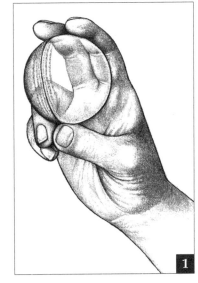

Conditions

Seam bowlers relish wickets with a degree of grip or purchase. This usually means a good covering of grass on a hard, fast surface, and ideally some dampness in the wicket. It is the latter that provides the 'juiciness' one sometimes hears bowlers talking about.

Some countries therefore favour seam bowlers, since the 'standard' wickets prepared there tend towards these characteristics, because of

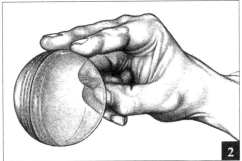

weather conditions or the materials used in the preparation of the playing square. English conditions have traditionally helped seam bowling, but perhaps surprisingly (given its reliance on pace in recent years), South Africa is a true seamer's paradise: grassy surfaces cover much harder tracks than those found in the United Kingdom. This is due to the harder undersoil used by South African groundsmen (usually bulli, a black clay) that makes the ball bounce.

Seam is still viable in countries with much rougher, drier pitches, such as Pakistan and the West Indies, but tends to be a factor only very early on in matches, before the moisture in the pitch has dried out and the ball's seam has been flattened through wear and tear.

The seaming action, with the first and second fingers imparting equal amounts of back-spin to the ball. Keep the wrist behind the ball to prevent the seam from wobbling in the air.

TROUBLESHOOTING GENERAL SEAM PROBLEMS

- **You're not getting any movement off the seam with the new ball:**

  You're not hitting the seam. Make sure it's leaving your hand with the seam vertical, and that you're flicking your wrist down behind the ball as it leaves.

- **It's seaming too much and the batsman isn't having to play:**

  If the batsman isn't having to play, you're bowling too short. Pitch it up, and the exaggerated movement you're getting will put serious pressure on him.

- **You're not getting any 'zip' and carry off the wicket:**

  Your rhythm is wrong.

  Or your wrist might be too loose. Freddie Brown, who captained England in the 1950s, thought that 'zip' came from action of the wrist, but there is no scientific evidence that backs this up. In fact, a stiffer wrist, flicking through with the arm rather than doing all the work at the point of delivery, seems to help the ball hit the deck harder, and therefore lift off more aggressively. Excessive wrist action or movement can also cause inaccuracy: when Allan Donald put his wrist into a delivery, it could go badly wrong (at pace!) down the leg side. Having said that, they don't get much nippier than South Africa's injury-blighted quick man Mfuneko Ngam, and he can bend his wrist back so that his fingernails almost touch his forearm.

  Another possibility is that you're gripping the ball incorrectly, either too tightly or loosely, or too deep in your fingers.

- **You lack bounce off the wicket:**

  Assuming you're not using a ball in very poor condition on a dusty, slow wicket, it seems most likely that you're simply not hitting the deck hard enough. Hit the deck! Your wrist has to come from behind the ball, and the ball should feel as if it's coming out of the barrel of a gun, rather than sliding out of your fingers.

- **The ball is straying down the leg side:**

  Your head isn't in the right place.

- **You're bowling too full and too short:**

  Your head isn't in the right place.

- **You're suffering from a general lack of accuracy:**

  Your head isn't in the right place.

2. SWING

The perfectly plotted and executed in- or outswinger, curving late in its flight and taking the edge or ducking back into the pads, is one of the most exhilarating experiences a bowler can ever hope for. When bowled well, with good control over line and length, it can be devastating, as the batsman is deceived into playing one line, only to have the ball swing off that line, leaving him groping.

The physics of swing and reverse swing are discussed in detail in the section on the science of swing on pp. 69–84, but it is important at this stage to have a basic understanding of why a cricket ball veers off its original line under certain conditions.

The ball is made of four quarters, separated into two halves by a proud (protruding) seam. Coaches who explain swing often refer to the seam as a rudder, but it is far more like the prow of boat, 'splitting' the air in front of the ball on its flight; and the two streams of air passing over the two sides of the ball travel at slightly different speeds. The side that is smooth and shiny will present less resistance to the air than the rough side: the resulting low pressure on that side of the ball will pull it in that direction and away from the high pressure. This manifests itself as swing.

This is why bowlers – and fielders – endlessly polish the same side of the ball. Indeed, it is the entire team's responsibility to 'groom' the ball in this way whenever it comes their way, dusting off any bits of grass or mud that might be clinging to

THE PITS

A local rule in South African cricket used to prohibit bowlers from using spit or sweat from their foreheads to shine or dampen the ball, so players resorted to using their armpits.

Naturally this saw an explosion of illicit substances (such as Vaseline and hair gel) being rubbed into armpits and then transferred onto the ball. Even regular underarm deodorants could be fairly sticky.

The end of South Africa's sporting isolation brought it into compliance with the international ruling, which allows for any amount of spit and sweat from the general area of the face to be applied, but bans the use of armpits (a blessing for bowlers and fielders who rub the ball with fingers and then put their fingers into their mouths!).

However, some of the old guard persisted in their devious and pungent ways. Spinner Pat Symcox was chief among the old guard who regularly popped the ball under his arm. These tactics went entirely unnoticed and unpunished on a tour of Pakistan in 1997/98, but a subsequent tour of Australia saw him very promptly pulled up short by the umpires.

the smooth side, and shining it as vigorously as possible. (Before lashing on the spit and sweat, remember that seamers prefer not to let the smooth side get too damp. Swing bowlers, on the other hand, need moisture to clean it and keep it shiny. Check what the bowler and the captain want in terms of 'ball-grooming' before you over-enthusiastically soak the ball!)

A prominent seam and a polished hemisphere only go so far. To swing the ball consistently and well you need:

- **a good basic action,** with the ability to vary it slightly, depending on the delivery you want to bowl
- **a good wrist position**
- **subtle differences in grip**
- **subtle variations on when you release the ball.**

Dennis Lillee, who could swing the ball with the best of them when the situation demanded it, was adamant about what a good swing bowler should do, and his explanation is an excellent starting point:

> The most critical part of swing bowling is the way you let the ball go from the hand. If this is not done with a high degree of precision, the ball either will not swing at all or will swing only a little and too early in its flight to be any great danger to the batsman. It starts with the grip of the ball, which should be made by contact of the index and middle fingers on the top of the ball and the thumb at the bottom. This contact should be towards the tips of the fingers and the thumb (what we call 'fingering' the ball), because if the ball is gripped too deeply in the hand, the critical control needed to send the ball away correctly may be lost. The hand should be directed behind the ball at the point of delivery and must not undercut on either side. The ball is sent away with a natural under-spin, and I believe the more under-spin imparted on the ball the later it will swing. The seam should remain vertical throughout the flight down the wicket (1982).

His view that under-spin or back-spin is crucial to swing bowling was illustrated by Australian swing bowler Bob Massie, who took 16 wickets in his first Test at Lord's in 1972. Lillee points out that when bowling, Massie managed to keep the seam absolutely steady for its flight, in no small part due to the large amounts of back-spin he put on the ball with a very whippy wrist action.

THE OUTSWINGER

There is simply no better ball to bowl at a new batsman than a fast outswinging yorker, or perhaps an outswinging half-volley on off-stump. This is a delivery that should be mastered by any bowler who wants to succeed in the game.

Tactically, the outswinger is intended to drag the batsman wide of his comfortable hitting zone, and to have him caught in the slips or at gully. However, many young or inexperienced bowlers make the mistake of getting carried away by the swing, and effectively bowling at the slips! This gives the batsman a pleasant over or two of being able to leave the ball and get settled. The ideal outswinger should be hitting off-stump or just curving away past it. The straighter you start it, the more chance you also have of pinning the batsman in front with an LBW shout, especially if he thinks it's a straight ball and tries to work it off his pads.

The grip

For a right-arm bowler facing a right-arm batsman, the seam is angled towards first slip, while the fingers point down the wicket. Remember that the ball will swing towards its rough half, so in this case, the rough side faces cover. The wrist is angled in towards the body and cocked backwards, while the side of the thumb rests on the seam under the ball.

The action

Outswing starts from 'behind' you. It takes some time to get the feel of when to release the ball for maximum effect, but basically the ball needs to be released from fractionally behind the ear. The hand and body must stay on line – driving through towards the target – and the follow-through must be full and complete.

Grip for outswinger

1. *The wrist is cocked for the outswinger – the idea is to snap the ball down from behind your head.*
2. *Here we exaggerate the 'round the pole' movement of the wrist and fingers.*
3. *The wrist snaps down as your fingers and wrist send the ball smoothly down the line of your arm and action.*

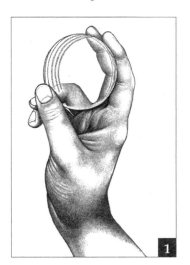

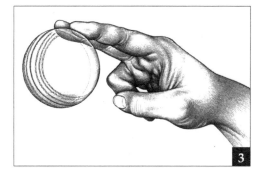

The best way of visualizing the correct arm and wrist action for the outswinger is to imagine putting a pole into the pitch on the bowling crease. Now try bowling around that pole, your arm coming round it on its right-hand side (left if you are a left-arm bowler). Turning your arm in this way will generate swing, but it is also easily spotted by the batsman, who will pick the delivery very early and score at will. So instead of doing it with the arm, go 'round the pole' with your wrist only.

THE INSWINGER

A good inswinger can be the most dangerous of all deliveries, if it is properly planned. For instance, it can be devastating if you've dragged the batsman outside his off-stump with a series of outswingers, and then shoot one back into his stumps or into his pads. As with an outswinger, you should generally be looking to hit off-stump, so start it outside off and let it swing in to hit the top of the stump.

Many bowlers find it easier to bowl inswing because the action does not have to be 'classical', but can be more open. Many young bowlers also take to it early on, thanks to a technical flaw: when they reach the stage in their development when they want to start bowling faster, they can develop an action that falls away early in the delivery stride. This is a natural (if unhelpful) inswing action, and one result is remarkably high numbers of inswing bowlers at lower levels of the game.

Having thus arrived at their action and ability to swing the ball almost by accident, these youngsters often see no reason to change: below a certain age, batsmen simply don't have the technique to cope with the ball coming in to them, and tend to leave the 'gate' open between bat and pad. This means there are wickets galore for the young inswing bowler, but as the batsmen who face him become more skilled, he becomes less and less effective. Eventually he has to learn to bowl the outswinger and correct his action. (At this point alarm bells should ring for the coaches of such bowlers, for it is here that the possibility of a mixed action creeping in is greatest, with all the attendant dangers – see above for how to prevent this.)

The grip

The seam is now angled towards leg-slip for the right-hander, and the flat pad of the thumb (rather than the side of the thumb) now rests on the base of the seam. This has the effect of cocking the wrist forwards.

The action

The inswinger is released 'in front' of the head, with the hand pushed over the ball, almost as a cobra's hood covers its head.

Grip for inswinger

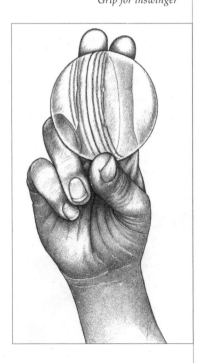

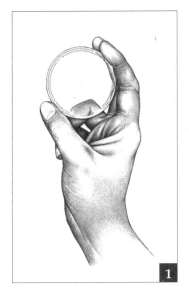

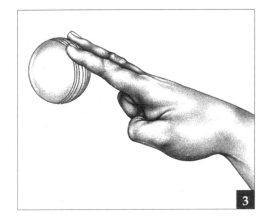

Visualize bowling 'round the pole' as you did for an outswinger, but this time move your arm around it clockwise (around it from the left, if you are a right-hander). Again, let the wrist do as much of the curving as possible, since your arm motion can be easily spotted; and since this is a more awkward and unnatural movement of your bowling arm, it takes less effort to simply move the wrist.

REVERSE SWING

When Pakistan's fast bowlers started getting the ball to swing in viciously and very late during the late 1980s and early 1990s, some of their victims cried foul. Not only were the likes of Imran Khan and Wasim Akram getting prodigious swing with the old ball, but they seemed to be swinging the ball in the opposite direction to where the seam was pointing. To the outraged – but ignorant – batsmen whose stumps and toes had been shattered, it all pointed to one thing: ball-tampering.

There was general uproar (as well as mystification and admiration) in cricketing circles. The fallout included the bitter and much-publicized libel case between Allan Lamb and Ian Botham on one side and Imran Khan on the other, as well as a legal run-in between Lamb and his former Northamptonshire teammate, Sarfraz Nawaz. The Englishmen lost their cases, and slowly the game's conservatives had to concede that the Pakistani bowlers had taken swing bowling to an entirely new level – and they didn't need leather-scuffing bottle-tops to do it either. Some rather more cynical commentators pointed out that it was those countries whose bowlers were the least able to extract reverse swing from their deliveries that had made the most noisy protests during the controversy.

1. The 'cobra head' is cocked, with the fingers forming the 'hood'.
2. The wrist does the work of pushing the ball 'round the pole' (here we have exaggerated the angle of the wrist for demonstration purposes).
3. The cobra strikes – this is not so much a snap of the wrist but a strong push, the wrist forming an extension of the arm.

The general explanation of reverse swing is fairly straightforward: a ball that has become extremely scuffed (from travelling around on a rough, grassless outfield) and has been continually polished with sweat on one side, will gradually become heavier on the side being polished. The delivery will then swing towards – rather than away from – that smoother side. The general principle may seem simple, but the practicalities of bowling reverse swing are anything but. It is not enough to pick up a battered ball and assume it will veer in late. The scratches and scuffs on the dry side of the ball increase the drag and allow it to duck in sharp and late when bowled at high speed, but exactly why this is so needs more careful explanation (see pp. 83–4). Moreover, the speeds necessary to get the ball to reverse are usually well beyond the ability of most bowlers. In addition, because the ball swings less dramatically than it does when swung conventionally, it needs to be bowled at a much fuller length; yet the yorker-length delivery is probably the most difficult one to bowl accurately: Waqar Younis was probably the best exponent of reverse swing the world has seen, and he was a master of the blisteringly quick inswinging yorker.

The advantages of being able to 'reverse' the ball into the right-handed batsman are obvious. Not only does it make the old ball a valuable tactical weapon, but it also enables the bowler to thoroughly bamboozle the batter, as he can now bowl what is essentially an inswinger with very little visible change of action.

The grip

The grip for bowling reverse swing is similar to that of an outswinger (see p. 57), with the shiny side pointed in the direction you want the ball to swing, and the seam pointed roughly at first slip. However, instead of having a vertical seam or rudder, the seam 'falls over' slightly. In other words, if you are right-handed, hold the ball as for an outswinger, and point the delivery at yourself. Looking at it as if you are a batter, roll the ball anti-clockwise by a few degrees. The seam should now be lying roughly from just outside your middle finger to roughly outside your thumb.

The action

Almost more than any other fast- or medium-paced delivery, reverse swing invites variation. There is no specific action that can be taught by coaches or learned by young bowlers: if you can make the ball reverse by slightly adapting your own action, don't do anything drastic to your basics. However, it seems that to reverse the ball into the pads, the action needs to be more round-arm (with a lower arm, rather than the vertical seamer's action or the upright slingy action of the in- and outswing specialists). The wrist also falls away slightly to the leg side at the moment of release – the snake-like 'wobble' seen in the wrist of reverse-swing maestros like Waqar and Darren Gough.

BALL-TAMPERING
AND REVERSE SWING

Since its arrival on the world stage was inextricably linked with allegations of ball-tampering, reverse swing has always struggled to shake off its reputation as a somehow devious or underhanded tactic. Many of the more conservative pundits continue to dispute its existence, demanding to know how reverse swing into the batsman differs from conventional swing. It is quite possible that some of this surprisingly acrimonious debate is still being fuelled by latent suspicions that reversing the ball is the preserve of cheats.

To make matters worse, these suspicions sometimes appear to have racist overtones. The problem is that the condition of the ball remains integral to reverse swing, and it is no coincidence that the tactic developed in countries with hard, dry outfields almost devoid of grass. As already explained, only a very scuffed ball, and one that has been constantly polished on one side, can reverse: so Pakistan provided ideal conditions for the phenomenon to emerge.

But it didn't help that the only Islamic Test-playing nation at the time was the one that introduced the phenomenon of reverse swing so spectacularly onto the international stage.

This was combined with the apparently 'miraculous' effect of reverse swing. The ball does not gradually begin to reverse – it does so suddenly, and in the hands of exceptionally skilled and speedy bowlers, spectacularly. Batting sides that felt comfortably settled in for a session would find themselves bustled out at humiliating speed once the ball began reversing. Hardliners like Ian Botham still insist that for a side to collapse from 250 for 2 to 280 all out, someone has to be cheating.

The scene was thus set for racial stereotyping that persists to this day, as reflected in the brouhaha over umpire Darrell Hair's declaration that the Pakistan side had tampered with the ball during a Test match with England in August 2006. This set a sequence of events in motion that led to the Pakistan team forfeiting the match.

However, one can't ignore the fact that many teams do tamper with the ball, speeding up the natural roughening process so that it can start reversing sooner. The prevalence of extremely powerful zoom lenses at international games has largely ended the practice among top teams, but some infamous occasions do stand out, not least for the controversy they caused. Imran Khan announced that early in his career, he'd taken a bottle-top to a ball; England captain Michael Atherton was caught on camera taking what he said was earth from his pocket, and rubbing it into the seam of the ball during a Test against South Africa; and South African captain Hansie Cronje caused indignation when he impaled a ball on the spikes of his boot during a one-day international game in Australia.

Probably the most significant impact the issue has had on the game has been to open up the debate on ball-tampering. In the case of the Darrell Hair incident involving Pakistan, both Angus Fraser and Colin Miller, the UK editor of Cricinfo.com, pointed out that when reverse swing won England the Ashes in 2005, its proponents were hailed as heroes and cricketing geniuses.

In a piece published in Britain's *Independent on Sunday* two days after the forfeited Test, Fraser courageously pointed out that in the course of his career, he had often helped along the scuffing of the ball, or run his finger-nails along the seam. He distinguished this kind of 'grooming' from the kind of actions involving resin, bottle-tops, and other more overt interventions. But if the ball was returned to him with a new scuff-mark after hitting the boundary boards, he saw no harm in 'roughing' up the sueded surface created in the process, as opposed to smoothing it down. He also pointed out that such behaviour, whether sanctioned by the Laws of the game or not, was covertly understood to be part of the game, and widely accepted as such. And more pertinently to the case of the forfeited England–Pakistan Test match, he noted that he had never been accused of ball-tampering for his actions.

TROUBLESHOOTING SWING-RELATED PROBLEMS

- **It's swinging without you trying to swing it, and you need to bowl a straighter line:**

  Hold it across the seam. If you're bowling with a two-piece ball and it's swinging uncontrollably, you're out of luck: two-pieces will swing no matter what you try! Four-piece balls can be stopped from swinging by changing your action – straighten up your arm and wrist.

- **It's swinging too much:**

  Change your line and stop making excuses!

- **It's not swinging at all:**

  If the problem is the conditions and not your action, then accept that it's just not going to swing, and start varying your bowling. Change the angle of delivery, and use the crease: bowl from close to the stumps, the middle of the crease and out wide.

- **Your inswingers are drifting down the leg side:**

  You're pushing it, not bowling it. Go back to the basics of your action, and ask your coach to watch you or (ideally) film you.

3. CUT

If there is one constant that runs through the game of cricket, it is that even the best-laid plans oft go awry. A track that was hard and bouncy on the first day skids through shin-high on the last day; the uncomfortable humidity that made the ball swing prodigiously in the first session develops into a still, bright, clear afternoon, ideal for batting. Sometimes even your careful homework can let you down: the batsman whom you had been told on good authority was helpless against outswing suddenly reveals a vicious late-cut and supreme judgement of where his stumps are.

As a fast or medium-pace bowler you need to be able to swallow your pride, take a step back, and reassess. Try to impose your will on the conditions, and you'll struggle. Rather ride the game as if you're surfing, keeping alert and mentally fluid.

If the ball has gone to sleep in your hand, or helpful cloud cover has evaporated, taking your ability to swing the ball with it, it's time to alter your approach. In this case, the cutter – whether an off-cutter or a leg-cutter – can be a more than useful substitute for swing.

Be warned: it takes years of practice to 'cut' the ball well at pace, but once mastered, it can be a devastating delivery, as it is effectively the fast bowler's version of a spinning delivery. Batsmen struggle enough with slow leg-breaks and off-breaks: a ball whistling down the pitch and zipping away to leg or off can be too much for many batsmen.

A cutter is also a very effective slower ball, since by running the fingers down the side of the ball (rather than flicking it out of the front of the hand), much of the momentum is bled away, without any change in the speed of the bowling arm.

The grip

Off-cutter: the seam is tilted towards the on side, with the fingers held slightly across the seam. As the ball is delivered, the fingers are brought down the side of the ball by the movement of the wrist. This will turn the ball in towards the right-handed batsman as it pitches.

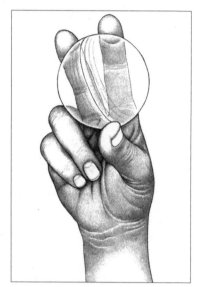

Grip for the off-cutter   *Grip for the leg-cutter*

Leg-cutter: the grip is the same as for the off-cutter, but the seam is now angled in the opposite direction, towards gully. There is less movement in the wrist, and more emphasis on letting the fingers 'fall' over the side of the ball. The faster this movement, the more purchase you're likely to get on the wicket.

The action

The basic action and grips for seam and swing still apply, but the bowler now alters the angle of the seam and pulls his fingers down the side of the ball, making it rotate sufficiently to grip and move after it pitches. (This is also one way of bowling an effective slower ball: the same action is employed, but the hand comes down the side of the ball, automatically slowing it down.) The bowler who intends to cut the ball has both the off-cutter and the leg-cutter at his disposal.

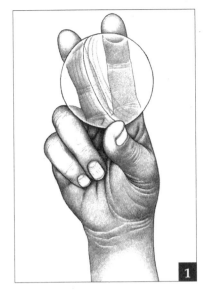 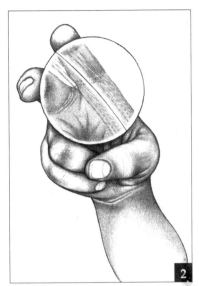 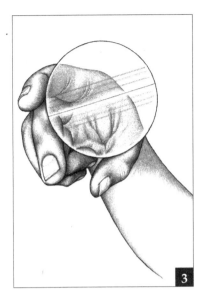

The action for the off-cutter: the fingers 'cut' down the outside of the ball, dragging down the seam to get maximum sideways revolutions (or to take the pace off, if you are attempting a slower ball).

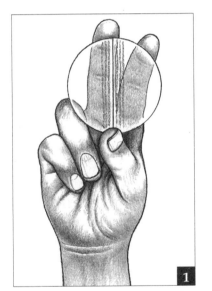 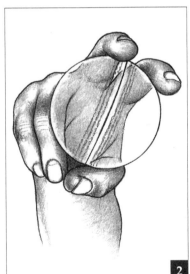 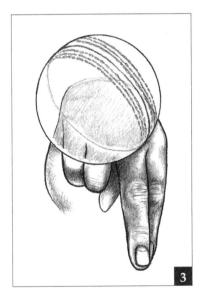

The action for the leg-cutter: the fingers 'cut' down the inside of the ball. Visualize allowing the ball to 'fall' forwards off the side of your fingers, and try not to put too much wrist into the delivery.

PRACTISING

No matter how brilliant a fast or medium-fast bowler might be, he cannot hope to get by on his talent alone, as a gifted batsman might be able to do. He must be superbly fit (at the elite level, we believe he needs to be as fit as any tri-athlete) and thus has little choice as to how hard he has to work on his game and fitness.

Indeed, it can sometimes seem as if the pace bowler has got a raw deal. While batting in the nets can be a relaxing or pleasurable exercise for batters, the bowler's standard practice is not much less intense than a match, at least in terms of the exertion he puts himself through in his run-up and action. On top of doing his share in the nets, he needs to practise his own specific skills, attend to his fitness routine, and then somehow find the time and energy for some batting practice as well.

Bowling practice is often repetitive and unstimulating. Trying to hit a single stump as many times as possible is an important drill, but a fairly mind-numbing one too. It is therefore important to find ways of keeping routines fresh and interesting. Coaches should recognize that bowlers are some of the most competitive people in any team, and should devise drills that take advantage of that desire to compete. For instance, the supremely competitive Richard Hadlee would challenge a bowling colleague to see who could hit a single stump the most times with a given number of deliveries.

Making repetition enjoyable is vital, because repetition and hard work are the only ways for the bowler to improve. Practise your repertoire of deliveries thoroughly, and always have an aim, whether to hit the top of off-stump or a particular spot on the wicket. (Off-stump is probably a better option, since different pitches and surfaces require different lengths, and you don't want to get used to one length, only to have it rendered useless by a very different surface in your next game.)

You will need patience and discipline. Practise one delivery at a time, for however long it takes until you are comfortable before moving on, and remember that all the world's greatest bowlers have spent months and years on their own as youngsters, simply bowling. Sometimes it was at batsmen, sometimes simply at a set of stumps. Clarrie Grimmett, the Australian spinner and teammate of Donald Bradman, practised his flipper for fifteen years before he used it in first-class matches!

THE FAST BOWLER'S KIT

There are two basic aspects to any fast- or medium-pacer's kit: clothing and boots. While the condition, fit and fabric of his clothing is important for comfort and optimum performance, it is his boots that can make or break him. Each cricketer has one crucial piece of equipment without which he would not only be completely ineffectual, but also in extreme amounts of pain. For the batsman, these are his pads; for the wicket-keeper, gloves. For the quick bowler, these are his boots.

These boots were made for bowling

Unfortunately, cricket boots have been neglected by the scientists who constantly advance and refine running shoes (whether long-distance shoes or sprinting spikes) and football boots. There are some fine manufacturers of cricket boots, but even they have tended to overlook the development of orthotics and shock-absorbing layers in favour of tried and tested techniques passed down more or less intact by nineteenth-century cobblers. And so the injuries continue as the volume of international cricket grows exponentially: ankles, shins, knees and hips damaged because of the economics of cricket, which do not reward investment in the scientific development of equipment.

Boots must be selected according to three important criteria:

1. COMFORT

Your feet will take a beating from bowling 20 overs in a day, and you can't afford blisters and bruised heels when running in.

2. SUPPORT

Ankles, arches and insteps need to be well braced; they should feel almost as if they have been strapped up by a physiotherapist. A low-cut boot may allow your ankle to turn in or out at the point of delivery, a serious injury waiting to happen. Similarly, you need to check whether the boot's manufacturer has developed anti-jarring inserts or supports: nine times your body weight is going through that single piece of equipment every time you land.

3. SPIKES

No fast bowler can risk a half-spike boot with rubber studs in the heel. This is entirely acceptable footwear for spinners, who need to pivot and who are landing with much less force than their fast-bowling colleagues; but the injuries resulting from a slip on landing (a heel stud not replaced, or a rubber cleat not gripping) can be severe. A full set of long spikes is not only a good idea in terms of a bowler's safety and effectiveness, but it is also a good tactical move: metal spikes very quickly destroy the pitch as bowlers follow through, creating rough on a good length outside the left-hander's off-stump. If you have a left-arm fast bowler in your team, even better: the rough is created outside off-stump, giving your spinner a big juicy target. Muttiah Muralitharan, Saqlain Mushtaq and Mushtaq Ahmed were all excellent spinners in their own right, but it didn't hurt their bowling figures to have left-arm pacemen Chaminda Vaas and Wasim Akram roughing up the pitch at the other end.

Modern professional cricketers will have at least three pairs of shoes in their coffin, while professional fast bowlers will probably have more. International quick bowlers often change their boots from session to session, so that they can conserve each pair (keeping the 'spring' in the sole and the ankle-support firm). Bob Woolmer recalled, 'I once had to give Lance Klusener a stern lecture on the importance of a well-stocked shoe cupboard when he tried to borrow another pair of boots just before a match – his own had split and he hadn't brought along a spare pair!'

Nevertheless, financial circumstances often dictate how much kit a player can have, and it is extremely unrealistic to insist that all players have at least two pairs of boots. Bob Woolmer remembered coaching bowlers in South Africa's impoverished townships who were lucky if they had one pair of boots – and these were often held together with duct tape and shoelaces.

However, if you are able to afford it, try to wear your new boots in at the beginning of the season, while keeping at least two other pairs you have already worn in reserve. It is vital for a fast bowler to have confidence in his footwear, to know that he can charge in and slam down his front foot at full throttle.

ROUGHING IT

Don't get carried away! Running on the pitch is forbidden, and if the umpire believes you are doing too much damage to your landing area, he is entitled to order you to change into rubber-soled boots without spikes, or to take you out of the attack entirely. Batsmen aren't exempt either. Those who are deemed to be deliberately running on the 'no-go' area of the pitch (to give their attack some purchase in the next innings) can have their runs cancelled and be similarly ordered to change footwear.

Clothing

The most important consideration here is that you should not stiffen up between overs or spells. If you are doing your job properly, you will be sweating freely, so try to wear cotton or wool, which maintain body heat and are better at preventing chills than synthetic fabrics. Keeping warm and loose is absolutely vital, and even in hot climates fast bowlers should wear a cotton vest or T-shirt under their cricket shirt. Quicks should also put on a jersey or jumper as soon as they finish an over, even if the sun is beating down. If there is even the slightest suggestion of a breeze, it is essential that they do so. Coaches of younger players should keep an eye out for this and nag if necessary.

THE SCIENCE OF SWING

Swing, whether in or out, early or late, has been part of cricket since overarm bowling became the norm over a century ago. Sometimes it is planned, as skilful professional or club cricketers get the ball to leave their hand just right. At other times, it is accidental, with schoolchildren or newcomers to the game experiencing frustration (and mystification) as the ball bends away down the leg side past a very unimpressed wicket-keeper.

And it is not only on the field that swing is an integral, if puzzling, part of the game. Show us a television commentary box or a back page dedicated to cricket or even just a lively debate around a water-cooler, and we'll show you a pundit worrying about the state of swing bowling, or hypothesizing about the core of the ball, or recalling the 'banana-balls' bowled by Ian Botham and Imran Khan in the 1980s.

And yet despite its prevalence in the game and the interest it has always generated among fans, there still seems to be no consensus over *why* the ball swings. In this section, we will explain the scientific facts and principles involved, and in so doing hopefully settle much of the debate.

The most common explanation given for why the cricket ball swings is based on the principle of friction. The theory is that the ball swings towards its rough side because the roughened leather provides more resistance to air flow, which causes friction on that side. The friction causes the rough side to travel more slowly through the air, the smooth side begins to 'overtake' it, and the result is a deviation towards the rough side.

It seems to make immediate sense, but it fails to explain why a new ball (which doesn't have a rough side) swings considerably more than an older ball. More importantly, it fails to take its assumptions to their logical conclusion. For instance, why does the ball, having started to deviate towards the rough side, then magically stop deviating? After all, by the time it reaches the batsman, according to the popular theory, it has deviated only to the extent that the seam is pointing towards the slips, after which it stops deviating.

In reality, if air friction were the sole cause of this deviation, the ball would continue to rotate on its horizontal axis until the smooth side faced forward and the rough side pointed back down the wicket towards the bowler. This would happen over a fairly short distance, and once the smooth side was facing forward, all further rotation or deviation would stop because the air friction on both sides of the ball would now be equal (see Figure 9 overleaf for a visual representation of how this would work).

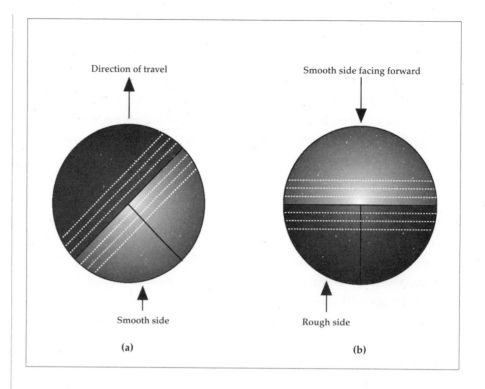

FIGURE 9: *If the swing of a cricket ball was caused by increased resistance to air flow over the rough side, the rough side would travel more slowly than the smooth side, causing the ball to rotate (a). This rotation would stop when the smooth side of the ball was facing forward (b). So the ball wouldn't swing, it would simply rotate on its horizontal axis, like the first quarter rotation of a spinning top.*

The traditional explanation, in other words, is flawed. The cricket ball does not simply swing because of friction. Rather, we need to look at the ball's wake, generated in the air around and behind the ball just as a ship creates a wake around and behind itself, and search for the answer in the changes the ball and bowler make to that wake. To do this, we also need to remember that air has mass: if air weighed nothing – for instance, if you were bowling on the moon – the ball would not swing.

THE BASICS OF AIR FLOW AROUND A SPHERE

To understand why a cricket ball swings under certain conditions, it is first important to grasp four fundamental concepts of the physics of ball motion through a medium like air. According to scientists, these are:

1. Patterns of laminar air flow around a sphere (such as a cricket ball) moving at different velocities through the air.

2. The development of turbulent flow in the wake of a sphere moving at increased velocity through air.
3. The boundary layer.
4. The critical Reynolds' number (Mehta et al., 1983).

As a bowler or coach, you will have encountered some and perhaps even many of these aspects already – friction, air flow, and so on – but the following explanations of these four points assume little prior knowledge: this is the physics of the ball's flight starting from scratch!

1. Patterns of air flow around a sphere (such as a cricket ball) moving at different velocities through the air

When any object moves through a medium like air, it experiences a force in the opposite direction to its forward movement. This retarding or drag force is known as wind resistance, and is caused by the energy required by the moving object to force its way between the molecules of air through which it is travelling. Since these molecules of air have mass, and are therefore attractive to other air molecules in their immediate vicinity, they resist any object trying to impose itself on this natural attraction.

Wind resistance increases as the square of the velocity (v^2) at which the object is moving, and is therefore most apparent at higher speeds. A measure of the magnitude of this retarding force can be gauged by comparing how far a sphere would travel in a vacuum in which there is no wind resistance, as occurs in space. Any object launched in space will continue moving at that speed forever or until it hits some obstacle.

FIGURE 10: *The path of air flow around a smooth sphere*

Even though a cricket ball is relatively small (compared to a soccer ball, for instance), air resistance has a substantial effect on the speed at which a fast delivery travels over even a distance as short as 18 metres. Thus, a ball leaving the hand of a fast bowler at about 160km/h (44,4m/sec) slows to about 138km/h (38,3m/sec) by the time it reaches the batsman. While some of this loss of speed will be due to the friction off the pitch as the ball bounces, most of it can be accounted for by the effects of wind resistance.

Figure 10 shows how air molecules move around a smooth sphere, in this case, a seamless cricket ball, travelling towards the batsman (at the top of the picture). The ball is viewed from above. (The reason why this particular cricket ball does not have a seam will be explained shortly.)

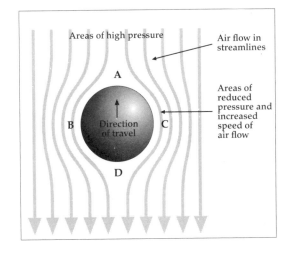

Areas of high pressure

Air flow in streamlines

Areas of reduced pressure and increased speed of air flow

A

B   Direction of travel   C

D

As the front of the ball (point A) moves through the air, it forces molecules around the sides of the ball (B – left side of the ball; C – the right side of the ball) until they meet again at point D at the back of the ball. The lines along which the air molecules move are known as streamlines. The flow pattern shown here is described as streamlined or *laminar* flow, since the streamlines remain parallel to each other, even though at the sides of the ball they are compressed closer to one another.

Of special interest to this discussion is the spacing of the streamlines in Figure 10 (p. 71): notice how they are wide in front and behind the ball, but increasingly compacted (although still parallel) along the sides of the ball at B and C.

These spaces represent the channels through which the air must flow on either side of the ball. Since the flow pattern in front of and behind the ball is steady (that is, the streamlines are laminar and equally spaced), then the air travelling in the narrowed channels around the sides of the ball must have sped up in order to return to the orderly air flow patterns in the wake of the ball. This means that the air must have travelled faster in order to cover the additional distance around the sides of the ball. Think of what happens when a river flows through a gorge or travels over rapids: the narrowness of the new channel causes the water to flow at a greater velocity compared to the slower pace of the water in the wider part of the river.

The greater velocity of the air travelling around the cricket ball (or the water flowing through the rapids), is caused by a difference in pressure as the air or fluid travels from an area of high pressure (in front of the ball or upstream of the rapids) to an area of low pressure (at the side of the ball or in the narrowest part of the channel), and then to an area of high pressure behind the ball (or in the water below the rapids).

Since the reduction in pressure caused by this increased rate of air flow is similar on both sides of the ball (the streamlines are exactly the same on each side of the ball) there is no side force on the ball. In other words, our seamless cricket ball, with its sides equally smooth, travels in a straight line.

2. The development of turbulent flow in the wake of a sphere moving at increased velocity through air

Figure 10 on the previous page shows the idealized (laminar) patterns of air flow around the surface of the cricket ball. But this idealized pattern can only occur if the air travelling closest to the ball surface (and which must therefore travel the greatest distance around the spherical surface of the cricket ball) has enough 'energy' to keep up with the slightly slower-moving air in the immediately adjacent air channel. The air molecules in this channel must not only travel faster, but they must also overcome the forces of friction between themselves and the very thin layer of air molecules which are adhering to the surface of the cricket ball and are therefore enjoying a free ride towards the batter – a privileged position that these adhering molecules are unwilling to relinquish. These frictional forces become increasingly important as the speed at which the sphere is travelling increases.

Thus, as the velocity of the delivery increases, the attraction between these two layers of air molecules increases. This means that more energy is required to ensure that the moving air is able to round the surface of the cricket ball in time to ensure that the flow remains laminar. However, eventually a speed is reached at which the ball is travelling so fast that the air travelling over the surface of the ball is unable to 'keep up' with the faster air flowing in the adjacent streamline next to it. As a result, the air at the ball's surface is no longer able to maintain the pace. Instead, it breaks from the surface, and stops flowing forward. Next, it begins to flow in the reverse direction, that is, towards the ball (Figure 11), before beginning to flow in a circular (eddying) pattern in the wake of the ball. Because these eddying currents are moving slowly, they produce an area of greatly increased pressure behind the ball, thereby producing an increased drag that slows down the delivery.

As in the previous diagram, the seamless ball is shown moving towards the top of the page/batter, as viewed from above. Since the air moving over the surface of the ball must travel both the furthest distance around the ball (A to D), and must also overcome the greater frictional forces caused by travelling over the surface of the ball, a speed is reached at which the air molecules in that layer are unable to keep up. Instead, they stop moving forward (D1) and reverse their direction (D2) before beginning the circular movement known as eddying (D3 to D6).

These eddying currents are the bane of all high-velocity sports, as they slow the progress of all fast-moving objects, be they racing-cars, cyclists, downhill skiers and even 100-metre sprinters. The principal focus of the study of aerodynamics is to try to reduce the development of these eddying currents around the surfaces of all fast-moving objects.

3. The boundary layer

As mentioned above, all objects exposed to air are coated with a thin layer of air that adheres to the surface. Much as a thin layer of water adheres to freshly washed hands and can be removed only by vigorous drying, high-speed air flow wrenches the surface layer of air from the object to which it is

FIGURE 11: *The development of eddying currents in the layer of air that travels immediately over the air attached to the surface of the cricket ball travelling at high speed*

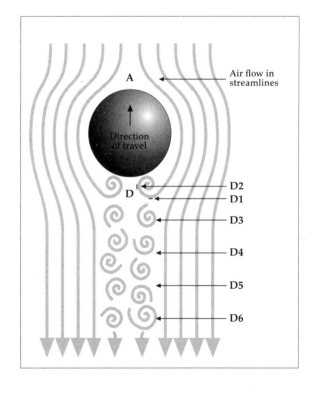

clinging. (The air is attracted to the surface of a cricket ball because of the attraction that the molecules of air have for the surface of any object.)

However, once the ball begins to move, the air immediately next to this layer must begin to flow at a higher speed than the air in the adjacent streamline in order to reach the back of the ball while maintaining laminar flow. But the closer the air is to the surface of the ball, the more energy must be expended in order to overcome the attraction for the resting air molecules coating the cricket ball. This layer of air adjacent to the cricket ball, and which is influenced by this effect, is known as the boundary layer. In other words, the boundary layer is that layer of air whose motion is affected by the presence of air molecules on the surface of the cricket ball. The effect of these surface molecules is to increase the amount of energy needed to drive air across them in the boundary layer. At some distance from the ball, this effect is lost and the air travelling around the ball beyond that distance is affected only by the surface geometry of the ball, but no longer by the effects of those surface air molecules (Figure 12).

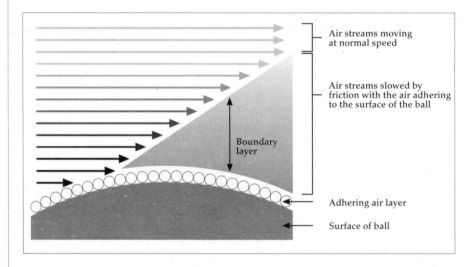

FIGURE 12: *Effect of the interaction of the adhering air layer and the boundary layer of air on air flow across a surface*

As described above, as the speed of the ball increases, the air travelling in this boundary layer has increasing difficulty keeping up with the air travelling in those streamlines beyond the boundary layer. Ultimately, a speed is reached at which the air travelling in the boundary layer is no longer able to keep up and, as a result, it separates, causing the eddying currents shown in Figure 13 on the opposite page. This is known as the separation of the boundary layer.

At low velocities, this separation occurs near the rear of the ball (Figure 13 on the left) but as the velocity of the delivery increases, this separation occurs closer to the front of the ball (Figure 13 on the right).

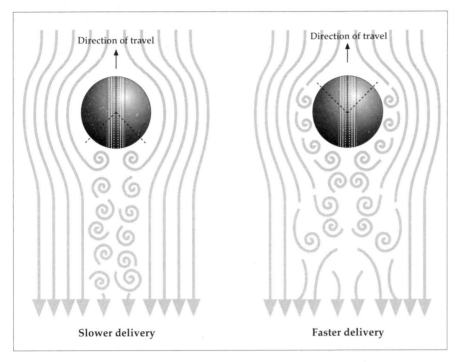

FIGURE 13: *Points of separation of the boundary layer at lower and higher speeds*

Note that the points of the separation on the adjacent sides of the ball, both sides of which are equally smooth, occur at adjacent points on the opposite sides of the ball. The point of boundary layer separation is not dependent purely on the velocity of the delivery, but also on the characteristics of the cricket-ball surface, as well as the prominence of the seam and the position of the seam relative to the direction of flight of the delivery.

As we will shortly discuss further, when there is a discrepancy in the point on the surface at which separation occurs, this produces a pressure difference in the streamlines of air travelling on either side of the ball, and the opportunity for swing develops.

4. The critical Reynolds' number

You now know that the drag caused by air resistance on a smooth sphere travelling through the air increases as the square of the velocity (v^2). This means that the drag on a delivery travelling at 40 milliseconds is four times greater than the drag experienced by a delivery travelling at 20 milliseconds.

However, for each sphere there is a specific critical velocity at which the drag due to air resistance is suddenly reduced, so that the sphere can suddenly travel much faster while producing the same drag.

The scientist Osborne Reynolds showed that a specific value, the so-called critical Reynolds' number, must be reached before this phenomenon can occur. Reynolds calculated that at a value over 200 000 (the critical value for the Reynolds' number, calculated from the equation given below), this drag suddenly drops.

The explanation for this phenomenon is that at the critical Reynolds' number, the air in the boundary layer begins to flow turbulently. As a result, air from the boundary layer and from the stream of air travelling immediately adjacent to the boundary layer begin to mix. This means that energy can be transferred from that layer to the boundary layer. The effect is that the air molecules can now travel faster in the boundary layer without losing as much velocity in overcoming their attraction for the surface air molecules. Because of this turbulent flow in the boundary layer, the energized boundary layer clings to the ball's surface for longer, separating only at the back of the ball, reducing the size of the wake of eddying currents trailing the ball. This reduces the pressure in the wake behind the ball, thereby reducing the drag and allowing the ball to travel faster.

The Reynolds' number (R) for any sphere is calculated as:

$R = 640vd$

in which v is the velocity of movement of the sphere in milliseconds and d is the diameter of the sphere in centimetres.

The diameter of a cricket ball is 7,2 centimetres, which means that the speed at which the critical Reynolds' number is reached is:

$$V = \frac{200\ 000}{640 \times 7,2} = 43,4\text{m/sec} = 156\text{km/h}$$

However, before bowlers start relishing the prospect of reduced drag should they crank up their pace to 156km/h and above, it should be pointed out that the Reynolds' number is dependent on the smoothness of the surface of this sphere. For this reason, it is difficult to give a precise critical Reynolds' number for a cricket ball (Daish, 1972), because the slightest surface roughness dramatically reduces the Reynolds' number for that sphere. This occurs because the roughness lowers the velocity at which turbulent flow develops in the boundary layer. In bowling terms, a lower Reynolds' number, brought about by surface roughness, means that the ball doesn't have to travel as fast as 156km/h to benefit from reduced turbulence.

Of course, if turbulent flow develops in the boundary layer on only one side of the cricket ball, the point of separation in the boundary layers on both sides of the ball will be different. When this occurs, conditions for swing are developed. The phenomenon of reverse swing especially is dependent on the reduction of the Reynolds' number on the side of an old cricket ball, one side of which is substantially rougher than the other side (this will be explained in more detail below).

The design of the golf ball is the most obvious practical example of the use of this effect to enhance the flight of the ball. The Reynolds' number for a smooth (undimpled) golf ball with a diameter of 4,12cm driven at a velocity of 70m/sec, as achieved by golfers like Tiger Woods, is only 79 000, well below the critical value of 200 000 needed to benefit from turbulent flow in the boundary layer.

But the effect of the dimpling on the surface of a golf ball is to reduce the critical Reynolds' number for the golf ball to velocities that are achievable by human golfers – i.e., velocities of between 50–70m/sec. As a result, the drag is reduced for at least some of the trajectory, allowing the ball to be hit further than would occur without the dimpling. Furthermore, the dimpling also increases the upward lift of the backward spinning golf ball as a result of the Magnus effect (covered in detail in the section on spin bowling on pp. 101–7).

FIGURE 14: *Turbulence in the boundary layer around a ball travelling at a speed above the critical Reynolds' number*

WHY THE BALL SWINGS

The phenomena described above may sound fairly complex and somewhat removed from the tussles that go on between batsman and bowler on the cricket field, but they form the foundations of the four vital ingredients necessary for the cricket ball to swing. These are:

- the height of the seam
- the speed of the delivery
- the stillness of the ball's vertical axis
- the angle of seam.

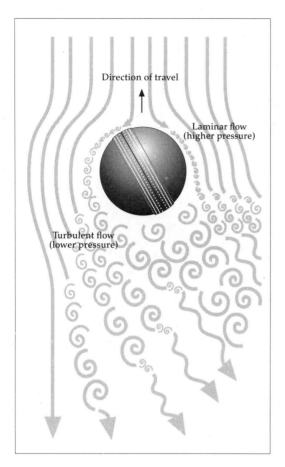

FIGURE 15: *The effect of the raised seam on the development of turbulent air flow around a cricket ball*

1. The height of the seam

As any cricketer knows, a new ball swings more than an older one. This is because the seam of a new ball stands proud (raised) above the surface of the ball. In this position, it is able to disturb the smooth flow of air in the boundary layer travelling on the side to which the seam is pointed.

As a result, turbulence is generated in the boundary layer on that side of the ball.

The first theoretical explanation of why the cricket ball swings seems to have been made by a Professor J.C. Cooke of the University of Malaya, who published his findings in the *Mathematical Gazette* in 1955. His explanation was reproduced in 1957 by R.A. Lyttleton, whose explanation was in turn repeated in Sir Donald Bradman's book, *The Art of Cricket*.

Cooke and Lyttleton proposed that swing is caused by the seam producing different flow patterns on either side of a cricket ball that is travelling above a certain critical velocity. Central to their argument is that the boundary layer must separate at different points on adjacent sides of the ball, since this produces the sideways force on the ball that is necessary to produce swing. This differential separation also produces an area of increased pressure in the wake of the ball (greater on one side) that will affect the further trajectory of the ball. In particular, the ball will travel away from the high-pressure area of turbulent flow.

But if the point of separation is the same on both sides of the ball, as shown in Figure 13 on p. 75, then the sideways forces on each side of the ball will cancel each other out, and the ball's future trajectory will not be affected other than to be slowed by the drag that develops in the wake of the ball.

However, if the separation point occurs at different points on the adjacent sides of the cricket ball, a pressure differential will be produced in the air surrounding the ball. This will produce a lateral (sideways) force on the ball, and this is what produces swing.

The boundary layer usually separates from the ball somewhere at or beyond the midpoints of each side of the ball, and the actual point of separation is determined by the velocity of the delivery – so that the faster the ball is travelling, the nearer it occurs to the front of the ball (Figure 13). Still, remember that if this separation occurs equally on both sides, the flight of the delivery will not be affected.

The key point is that a difference in separation points can be produced by having laminar flow on one side of the ball and non-laminar or turbulent flow on the other side. As illustrated in Figure 10 on p. 71, laminar flow is characterized by smooth tiers of air flowing one on top of each other in parallel streamlines. Turbulent flow, by contrast, sees chaotic movement throughout each streamline, as shown in the areas beyond the point at which the boundary layer separates in Figures 13 and 14.

However, here we encounter a paradox: laminar flow causes the boundary layer to separate from the ball *earlier* than is the case with turbulent flow. This is because during turbulent flow, energy is borrowed from the air in the adjacent streamline, and this extra energy allows the air to travel faster and so stick to the side of the ball for longer.

So one mechanism of producing swing is to produce laminar flow on one side of the ball and turbulent flow on the other. Since the pressure in air moving turbulently is lower than in air moving in laminar flow, a pressure differential is produced which sucks the ball towards the area of lower pressure – the side of the turbulent flow. The effect of a prominent seam, as found in cricket balls, is that it helps produce turbulent flow on the side of the ball to which the seam is pointing (see Figure 15).

- To illustrate this with a practical cricketing example, consider an outswing delivery to a right-handed batsman, with the seam of the ball aimed towards the slips (Figure 16). As the seam strikes the onrushing air on its left side, turbulent flow is produced in the boundary layer so that the point at which the boundary layer separates on the left side of the ball

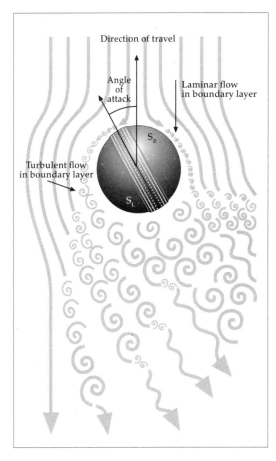

FIGURE 16: *The effect of the seam in producing swing away from a right-handed batsman. This occurs at delivery speeds of 80–120 km/h.*

(S_L) moves further to the rear on that side. In contrast, the absence of the seam on the right side of the ball striking the onrushing air allows laminar flow to occur on the right-hand side of the ball. But since laminar flow separates earlier from the ball's surface than turbulent flow does, the boundary layer separates closer to the front of the ball on the right side of the ball (S_R). This is because the turbulent flow 'borrows' energy from the streamline adjacent to the boundary layer, and this allows the boundary layer to 'stick' to the ball surface for longer. The roughness of this surface also reduces the Reynolds' number required to produce turbulent flow, further encouraging the development of turbulent flow. A ball with a rough surface on the left side and a smooth surface on the right will swing more, since the rough left side will allow the development of non-laminar flow at lower bowling speeds than a ball with two shiny sides.

The difference in the separation points on adjacent sides of the cricket ball generates the sideways force that produces the swing. Calculations suggest that the force produced by the difference in separation points caused by a new seam is sufficient to produce sideways movement of up to 50cm during the approximately 16 metres of the cricket ball delivery (Bown and Mehta, 1993; Barton 1982). Add half a metre of swing caused by the seam alone to another half-metre created by the bowler's action, the overhead conditions, and the pace of the ball, and you have the classic 'banana-ball', speared in at middle-stump and veering away towards the slips. Note that the optimum angle of attack – the angle between the direction of flight and the direction of the seam – needs to be between 20–40° for optimum swing to occur.

2. The speed of the delivery

As already described, in order to swing away from a right-hander, laminar flow must be preserved on the right side of the ball (Figure 16). For this to happen, the surface on that side of the ball should be smooth, and it must be travelling at the correct speed. The Reynolds' number will determine at what speed the air flowing around a spherical object will become turbulent: for a cricket ball with a smooth surface, this will be at about 112km/h. At higher speeds, the flow on the smooth right side of the ball in Figure 16 will become turbulent, and the boundary layer separation point on the smooth side will move further towards the back of the ball so that the separation points become more similar, reducing swing. This explains why very fast bowlers are unable to swing the ball as much as medium-paced bowlers.

It is also sometimes suggested that the swing that occurs late in the flight occurs because the ball's velocity slips below the critical velocity predicted by the Reynolds' number, so that laminar flow returns on the smooth side of the ball. However, once turbulent flow has developed, it is improbable that it will revert to laminar flow, except at significantly low speeds. Another explanation is that the amount of swing produced by the lateral force is cumulative, producing an exponential parabolic flight path (i.e., a steadily accumulating amount of swing that only becomes visible to the naked eye in its later stages) so that most of the lateral movement will seem to occur just as the delivery approaches nearer to the batsman (Bartlett et al., 1996).

SWING IT INTO THE WIND?

Since most bowlers believe that swing is generated simply by angling the seam and allowing the rough side of the ball to generate friction, they sensibly assume that bowling into a strong headwind will generate more swing. But they're wrong. Remember that swing depends on the ball's speed *relative to the air through which it is passing*. Bowling with the wind reduces the speed of the delivery relative to the air through which it is travelling, which increases a fast bowler's chances of generating swing. Likewise, bowling into the wind increases the relative speed of the ball, meaning that the quick bowler is less likely to get the ball to swing – as explained above.

3. The stillness of the ball's vertical axis

All young bowlers should work hard at getting the ball to leave their hand in exactly the right position, but in the case of seamers, this is not only for reasons of accuracy and pace, but also to enable the ball to swing. The swinging delivery should be bowled with as little 'wobble' around its vertical axis as possible: the less wobble in the seam (in other words, the less the seam veers from third slip to leg gully and back), the more laminar will be the flow on the smooth side of the ball.

While the position of the wrist and the bowler's action are integral to keeping the ball stable on its vertical axis, back-spin is also important: a flick of the fingers down the back of the ball at the point of delivery helps to stabilize the ball. The optimum back-spin speed is usually between 11 and 14 revolutions per second (Mehta et al., 1983).

Dennis Lillee believes that when the seam has been flattened and the ball has lost its smoothness, swing can still be generated as a result of the difference in relative smoothness between the two sides of the cricket ball. However, the seam should now face forward. The Australian paceman also holds that the more back-spin imparted on the ball, the later it will swing. (For more of Lillee's advice on generating swing, see the section on fast and medium-pace bowling.)

4. The angle of seam

The seam must maintain an optimum angle of attack (see Figure 16) throughout the delivery. Mehta et al. (1983) showed that maximum swing is produced at a ball velocity of 112km/h when the angle of attack is 20° and the rate of back-spin is between 11 and 14 revolutions per second.

FURTHER MYSTERIES OF SWING

What about the weather?

It is one of cricket lore's oldest and most familiar wisdoms that the ball is more likely to swing in humid or cloudy conditions, but there is still no explanation for why this is the case. Indeed, most puzzling is the fact that a humid atmosphere is less, not more, dense than a dry atmosphere, and should therefore be less, not more, conducive to generating swing. One suggestion is that the humidity either swells the seam, although this is unproven (Mehta et al., 1983), or that it interacts with the varnish of the ball, making it easier for the bowler to grip and thus to impart the ideal amount of back-spin.

Matthew Turner (2002) from Brisbane, Australia, offers a different theory. He suggests that humidity must be separated from the effect of temperature. Even though the humidity can be 100% in Brisbane, the ball hardly ever swings on a hot summer's day. This suggests that heat negates the effects of humidity.

Turner suggests that this may be because heat increases turbulence in the air near the pitch through which the ball is travelling. He suggests that heat produces micro-turbulence in the region of the (hot) pitch surface, which is not recognized as its effects are too slight to be noticed.

His theory is that when the pitch is warm, because the sun is shining without cloud cover, the micro-turbulence that develops in the air immediately above the pitch interferes with the development of turbulence in the boundary layer on the rough side of the cricket ball, and which is so crucial for the development of swing.

His corollary is that when there is overhead cloud, there is less direct sun on the pitch and therefore less heat and less micro-turbulence in the air through which the ball travels. As a result, conditions are more favourable for swing. According to his theory, the ball will swing when the pitch is as cool or colder than the surrounding air.

He also suggests that this might explain why humidity apparently makes the ball swing; this is less likely to be the effect of humidity than the effect of heat on air movement directly above the pitch.

Turner concludes with the advice: 'Look at the weather forecast for the whole game, and look for the best swing conditions if you have swing bowlers, and always bowl if you win the toss after overnight rain' (2002, p. 49).

Or maybe it's the balls

There is another aspect to swing bowling. Since the retirement of Wasim Akram and Waqar Younis, the international arena has seen a remarkable scarcity of swing bowlers, and even those two stellar Pakistanis were almost unique in their day in their ability to make the ball duck in late in its flight. England's Matthew Hoggard had some impressive returns against South Africa and Australia in 2004 and 2005, but many pundits claim that the art of swing bowling is rapidly being lost as real pace and miserly line and length become the norm for the seam bowler.

Even Sir Alec Bedser (regarded by many as the best swing bowler in the history of the game) held a pessimistic outlook about the future of the art: 'We [England] have gradually produced a crop of bowlers who cannot bowl swingers,' he said, an opinion shared by the Test and County Board of England whose assessment in 1993 was that 'the general quality of swing bowling in the [English] domestic game is as low as it has ever been' (Bown and Mehta, 1993).

These criticisms are based on the assumption that a cricket ball will always swing when exposed to the aerodynamic factors already discussed, and that modern bowlers are simply not managing to master the necessary skills to impose those factors on their deliveries. But this ignores the fact that cricket balls themselves have changed considerably in construction from those used even as recently as the 1980s, when Ian

Botham and Imran Khan were swinging the ball to such effect. The Kookaburra balls used today are arguably completely different from those Bedser might have used. It is certainly possible that their design and construction might negatively affect their potential for swing. Having levelled a charge of 'they don't make them like they used to' at modern bowlers, pundits may do well to shift that accusation onto the balls being used. In his 1998 autobiography, Wasim Akram argued that the Reader ball, which he used to such devastating effect during the 1990s, aided reverse swing far more than either the Duke or the Kookaburra ball. He noted that when he captained the Pakistan side, the toss he was most keen to win was for the choice of which make of ball to use during a Test match!

So it seems that further research is needed into the current methods of constructing cricket balls, and how these methods and materials might affect swing.

THE AERODYNAMICS OF REVERSE SWING

The ability to swing the ball in the opposite direction to which it is expected to travel (i.e., in which the seam and roughened side of the ball suggest it should go out) was first perfected by Imran Khan and other Pakistani fast bowlers. Dr Rabi Mehta, who opened the bowling with Imran for the first cricket team of the Royal Grammar School in 1972, has offered the currently accepted explanation of how reverse swing is generated (Bown and Mehta, 1993).

Mehta recalls that sometime after 1980, Khan had informed him that he had noticed that, on occasion, a new ball would swing in the direction opposite to that which was intended. The explanation of Bown and Mehta (1993) is that such 'reverse' swing is possible if the speed at which the new ball is delivered is sufficiently fast.

They suggest that at speeds between about 80 and 120km/h, the seam of the ball is able to produce the turbulent flow on the seam side of the ball as shown in Figure 5.16. However, as the speed rises above 120km/h, the point at which the laminar flow on the smooth side of the ball begins to separate moves towards the front of the ball. Eventually the ball is travelling so fast that the boundary layer strips even before it strikes the seam. What this means is that the seam is now acting as a ramp, directing the air on that side away from the ball, causing the boundary layer to separate earlier on the seam side of the ball – the opposite of what normally occurs in an outswinging delivery (Figure 17). This is thought to occur at speeds of 130–145km/h. When this occurs, the sideways force on the ball is reversed so that the delivery bowled as an outswinger, actually swings in (Figure 17 on the left).

Bown and Mehta (1993) suggest that the next advance produced by the Pakistani bowlers was the discovery that reverse swing – inswing achieved with a ball bowled with an outswing action and the seam of the ball directed at the slips – could be

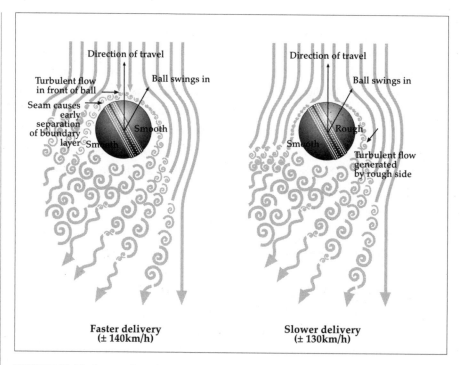

FIGURE 17: *The impact of speed and the condition of the ball in bowling reverse swing*

achieved at lower speeds if the rough surface of the ball was bowled facing forward (Figure 17 on the right). The effect of the roughened side is to produce turbulent flow more easily at the front of the ball. Furthermore, the rougher the surface, the more marked this effect. As a result, the boundary layer separates further to the back of the ball, thereby causing low pressure on the right side of the ball – conditions that favour inswing, i.e., reverse swing.

Bown and Mehta (1993) conclude that the key to conventional swing is to have one side as smooth as possible, whereas the key to reverse swing is to have one side as rough as possible. A ball with one very smooth and one very rough side provides the bowler with the possibility of producing either out- or inswing with the same action.

IN THE END, THE MYSTERY REMAINS

In the final analysis, all these theories and hypotheses are exactly that: to our knowledge, no-one has yet shown conclusively (using a swinging delivery produced by a swing bowler in a real match) that the factors discussed above provide exclusive explanations for why the ball does or doesn't swing. The explanations given here are based on solid principles of physics, but because it is not yet possible to measure all these variables on a swinging delivery out of doors, the real contribution to the generation of swing of each of the listed theoretical factors remains largely unproven.

SLOW BOWLING

Slow bowling is one of the art forms of cricket. Watching a good spinner, with his leisured and graceful approach and delivery, performing his repertoire of tricks and traps, is to remember that cricket is not just about brute force and pace.

By the 1980s, the art of slow bowling had been all but lost, after two decades of absolute domination by pace attacks. Even those who kept the flame of spin dimly burning – such as India's Bishen Bedi, Pakistan's Abdul Qadir and England's Derek Underwood – were often eclipsed by the murderous quick men; three or four intricately conjured wickets, gained with patience and guile, would be overshadowed instantly by one fiery short ball taking the glove and looping to gully. The consensus seemed to be that spin was in dire straits, perhaps even dying out.

The prospects looked even grimmer with the advent of one-day cricket. Defensive bowling against batsmen who were putting a lower price on their wickets – and therefore far more willing to attack – made all but the best spinners a liability. The final nail in the coffin was hammered in by groundsmen, now equipped with more sophisticated irrigation systems and under pressure to prepare impressively green pitches for television consumption. The damp uneven pitches known to spinning maestros of yesteryear such as Bill 'Tiger' O'Riley, Clarrie Grimmett, Jim Laker, Richie Benaud and Lance Gibbs were a thing of the past.

By 1990, spinners had become luxury selections, a safe option if the four pace men were likely to find the going a little heavy, but certainly not likely to roll a side over with five or more wickets. Some fine finger-spinners did their best to prove the critics wrong, with the likes of Tim May (Australia), Phil Tufnell (England) and Roger Harper (West Indies) regularly chipping in or mopping up tail-enders; but they seldom got the fields they wanted, and if they failed to take wickets, they (or their selection) would come under fire by their media.

In the general climate of gloom and under-achievement in the world of slow bowling, few eyebrows were raised when a young Australian leg-spinner had a nightmare debut at Sydney in 1992 – Ravi Shastri along with the rest of the Indian team left him with the singularly unimpressive figures of 1 for 150. But his captain, Allan Border, along with Australia's selectors, saw something India's batsmen hadn't. One year later Mike Gatting and the cricketing world watched dumbstruck as a viciously spun leg-break drifted outside the Englishman's leg-stump, pitched, and ripped past the outside edge of the bat to hit off-stump. Shane Warne had arrived: brash, iconoclastic, larger and louder than life. Almost overnight, spin (and specifically wrist-spin) became not only fashionable, but glamorous. Young cricketers began dreaming of being the next Shane Warne rather than the next Curtly Ambrose or Allan Donald.

But any renaissance relies on the simultaneous convergence of talents and circumstances, and Warne's emergence coincided with the arrival on the international stage of three exceptional spinners from Asia: India's Anil Kumble, Pakistan's Mushtaq Ahmed, and Sri Lanka's Muttiah Muralitharan (who, although an off-spinner, gets as much turn as a wrist-spinner). By the mid-1990s, the idea of the slow bowler as strike bowler had gained widespread acceptance, and a kind of cricketing arms race had developed around wrist-spin, as each Test-playing country searched desperately for its own match-winning leg-spinner.

Some countries found temporary solutions to the perceived 'leg-spin gap'. South Africa unearthed teenager Paul Adams, while Zimbabwe had some success with Paul Strang, but others were less lucky. England's brief flirtation with Chris Schofield ended in acrimony and failure – not surprisingly, given the lack of development of spinners and the green, lush pitches in England – while the West Indies' attempts to develop Dinanath Ramnarine and Rawl Lewis sadly came to nothing.

Today spin is surprisingly healthy, given the prevalence of one-day cricket and spin-unfriendly pitches, but its survival should not be taken for granted. Producing match-winning slow bowlers is not a question of money: England and South Africa, two relatively well-resourced cricketing countries, have shown themselves to be incapable of consistently producing even moderately good spinners, let alone strike bowlers; while Sri Lanka, one of the poorest Test-playing countries, has produced not only the phenomenal Muralitharan, but also the extremely capable Upul Chandana. Similarly, Zimbabwe managed to produce Ray Price, a useful finger-spinner, even in the midst of that country's political and economic implosion.

Financial infrastructure, therefore, would seem to have little effect on the emergence of good slow bowlers. Instead, what they need is a supportive school and club system (one in which coaches and captains do not panic when they see their spinners getting hit out of the attack, and in which fielders have the skills to hang onto chances at short leg or in the deep); a fair number of pitches that offer them more than the slick grassy surfaces in vogue throughout the Anglophone cricketing world; and a public appreciation of their craft. Thanks to Warne and Muralitharan, this final requirement is spreading rapidly, but the first two can easily be neglected, fatally undermining one of the game's loveliest arts.

By the mid-1990s, the idea of the slow bowler as strike bowler had gained widespread acceptance, and a kind of cricketing arms race had developed around wrist-spin, as each Test-playing country searched desperately for its own match-winning leg-spinner.

RICHIE BENAUD ON THE ATTRIBUTES OF THE SUCCESSFUL SLOW BOWLER

Not many people can claim to have reached the top of their field in two long careers, but when Richie Benaud retired from broadcasting in 2005, he signed off on a working life in which he rose to eminence as the finest wrist-spinner of his era, became Australia's leading all-rounder of the 1960s (as well a fine and insightful captain), and then went on to entrench himself as the doyen of cricket commentators.

For Benaud, there are five key elements that a bowler must make part of his life and his game if he is to be a successful spinner. These five pointers are taken from the Appendix to Benaud's *Anything but ... An Autobiography*:

1. Patience: Bowling is a tough game and you will need to work on a batsman with your stock ball, sometimes for several overs, before putting a plan into action....

If you take a wicket on average every ten overs in Test cricket, you will have a better strike rate than O'Reilly, Grimmett and Benaud. If you take a wicket on an average every eight overs, you will have the best strike-rate of any modern-day Test bowler, fast or slow.

2. Concentration: Anything less than a hundred per cent concentration running in to bowl is unpardonable. The spot on the pitch where you want the ball to land should be the most important thing in your mind from the moment you turn at your bowling mark.

If someone offered you $20 000 to throw a ball and hit an object nineteen yards away... would you, as you were throwing, look at someone standing close by, or at some other object?

3. Economy: This is a war between you and the batsmen.

Is there some very good reason you want to allow them more than two runs per over?

4. Attitude: Calm, purposeful aggression and a clear mind are needed, plus a steely resolve that no batsman will ever get the better of you over a long period of time....

In other walks of life you want to be mentally strong and on top of the opposition. Is there some particular reason why this should not be the case with your battle with the batsmen?

5. Practice: All practice should be undertaken with a purpose.

You think hard before doing most other things, why should you allow cricket practice to be dull and boring? (1998, p. 284).

THE BASIC PRINCIPLES OF SPIN

The fundamental strategies and techniques of spinning the cricket ball mirror almost exactly those of fast and medium-pace bowling. Everything we have discussed about line, length, bowling with rhythm, picking a target (whether on the pitch or the top of off-stump) and the need for patience, apply as much to spin bowling as they do to seam.

However, there is a profound difference between the two schools of bowling. The fast bowler needs speed through the air, but it is as important – if not more so – that he masters control of lines and lengths, changes of pace, and learns to move the ball off the seam or through the air.

The spinner needs strategic attributes too, but above all else, he must be able to do one thing: spin the ball. Turn – masses of it – must be his aim above all else. He must want to 'turn it square' – make it kick to the leg- or off side at 90° – and he must dream of bowling batsmen around their legs or of getting the ball to skip into middle-stump from two feet outside off-stump, before he even begins to experiment with flight, drift and quicker, flatter deliveries.

So the whole object of the grip and action of the slow bowler is no longer to deliver the ball with the full force of the bowler behind it, but rather to propel it down the wicket in such as way that it rotates rapidly through the air. Whether it rotates clockwise, anti-clockwise, end over end, or around its horizontal axis, and how fast it spins in any of those directions, depends on how it is released and on which kind of bowler has let it go. Sometimes this is done by spinning the ball with fingers, sometimes with a swift rotation of the wrist; the body is always swivelled with the front foot used as a pivot; but whichever method is used, the ultimate goal is 'fizz', that vicious kicking spin that can be heard as the ball hisses through the air just before pitching.

Revolutions are king, but the thoroughbred match-winner needs more, and without a doubt the most crucial among the slow bowler's secondary array of weapons is accuracy. No matter how far he can turn the ball, or how many variations he has, if he is not accurate, he will not be much use. Landing one ripping, fizzing delivery on the perfect spot before sending down five long-hops and full-tosses is a recipe for disaster. Indeed, the career of South Africa's Paul Adams was truncated largely because of his penchant for delivering one 'four-ball' per over, whether an over-pitched googly or a Chinaman dragged down short. Again, Warne and Muralitharan are the ideal models: both have the ability to land a ball on the same spot over after over, or slowly change their line while keeping a single length, working a batsman across his stumps.

The third attribute of world-class slow bowlers is absolute control over the pace of the ball. Batsmen are opportunists, and even those out of their depth against most bowling will quickly recognize that a spinner is bowling at one pace, and will have plenty of time to come down the wicket or play back to predictably looping balls. The slow bowler must be able to alter his pace in tiny, almost unnoticeable increments, either by slowing down and adding more flight, or by speeding up and spearing the ball in flatter.

THE BOTTOM LINE: SPIN OR ACCURACY?

We don't want to give young bowlers an excuse not to work on their control and accuracy, but in the final analysis spin will always be more important than accuracy. The bowler who spins it a long way will always take wickets, because batsmen will still get out to your long hops. But if you bowl inaccurately and don't spin the ball either, you'll get smashed. Master both, and you have the potential to have a profound effect on the game.

Finally, the good slow bowler must recognize that skill and success do not come overnight: while pace bowlers are born, the spinner is a self-made man. He matures later in his career than almost any other cricketer, and that maturity depends largely on how solid his confidence is. An early setback – or, worse, a series of early setbacks – often sees young spinners give up entirely, turning instead to seam bowling or batting. All too often spinners are used as change bowlers, or stuck on for an over before tea. Alternatively, they get a hiding in their first match, and are promptly whipped off by their captain or coach, getting the message loud and clear that they cannot be trusted to explore their new craft. (Imagine if Allan Border had done this to Shane Warne after the latter's fiasco against India in 1992.) If you enjoy spinning, stick to it: with plenty of hard work, and a little luck (a misjudged sweep, a well-held catch in the deep), you will develop the confidence and the skills you need to be successful.

The ideal attributes of a spinner are therefore:
- **prodigious spin**
- **accuracy**
- **the ability to change pace subtly**
- **a willingness to practise and persevere.**

THE ART OF DECEIT

It is not a bad rule, though subject to variations, that you can bowl a batsman out in the first three overs… and after that, you have to trap him.

Learie Constantine, *Cricket and I*, 1933

Fast bowlers force batsmen into errors by beating their reflexes or by unnerving them with the threat of physical injury; seam and swing bowlers beat their man by getting him to commit to a certain line, and then moving the ball off that line too late for the batsman to adjust. But without pace, either of the dangerous or the reflex-beating variety, the bowler is completely vulnerable to the batsman's reactions. Batsmen have to wait for the spinning ball to arrive at the best of times: bowl even slower, giving batsmen even longer to plan their shot, and the result is usually wrecked bowling figures and an early posting to the outfield.

The spinner, therefore, must rely almost entirely on deceit, on persuading the batsman to play the wrong line or length, or to play too early, or not early enough. As a result, spinners have developed their skills and strategies to deceive batsmen about three aspects of the delivery:

- **The exact place on which the ball will land:** Slow bowlers strive to land the ball fractionally further from the batsman playing forward than he expected, or closer to the batsman playing back. Alternatively, they look to deceive the batsman about the line on which the ball will eventually pitch, either by getting the ball to drift (see the discussion of the Magnus effect on pp. 101–7) or by subtly changing their point of delivery on the bowling crease.

- **The exact time at which the ball will arrive:** The human brain cannot accurately calculate the exact trajectory of a delivery that spends a part of its flight coming directly towards the eyes, or that travels above the horizontal plane of the eyes. Hence flight and subtle changes of pace go a long way in bamboozling batsmen.

- **What the ball will do after it pitches:** This final point is the Pandora's Box all spinners love opening, and which makes spin such an absorbing spectacle. Whether the ball will bounce viciously at the gloves like a fast Anil Kumble leg-break (or shoot up at the splice like an even faster Shahid Afridi leg-break!), or squat and go straight like Warne's infamous flipper of the early 1990s, depends on the skills the bowler has developed, the strength of his fingers, the integrity of his action, and the keenness of his mind, allowing him to adapt his technique to the pitch conditions.

And it is those skills that we will now explore. Hopefully, they will point you in a direction that will allow you to open your own Pandora's Box, letting the contents loose on a generation of groping, leaden-footed batsmen.

Flight

> *The truth is that no great batsman is likely to be bothered by break, save on unplayable pitches, if he is in no trouble while the ball is coming through the air. [Wilfred] Rhodes gets his men out before the ball pitches; spin with him is an accessory after the act of flight – flight which disguises the ball's length, draws the batsman forward when he ought to play back, sends him playing back when he ought to come forward, and generally keeps him in a state of mind so confused that in time he begins to feel it might be a mercy to get out. Against Rhodes, no long innings has ever been played that did not at the end find the batsman intellectually a little worn and weary.*
>
> Neville Cardus, *A Summer Game*, 1929

The ability to develop and master flight, or 'loop', as it is often called, is an added bonus to any spinner. Anyone who has ever seen a tennis ball dip suddenly towards the ground after a fierce top-spin forehand will understand the phenomenon: loop is created by imparting fierce spin, usually something akin to top-spin (rather than just by rolling the ball out), allied to a quick bowling-arm action and a slow front-arm action.

Of course there are as many varieties of loop as there are gifted slow bowlers. Top-spin will cause a ball to hang in the air before dropping more steeply (and therefore bouncing higher) than the batsman expects; back-spin hurries the ball through lower and fuller, and also keeps low after pitching, thus 'skidding' on to the batsman; while side-spin creates 'drift' in the flight of the ball before it pitches, sending it drifting laterally across the pitch, either into or away from the batsman. This last variation of loop can be particularly devastating if the drift happens in the opposite direction to that in which the ball spins, for instance, the leg-break that drifts off the straight into the pads of the right-hander and then spins across him towards his off-stump.

FLIGHT SCHOOL
Coaches and young bowlers, whether finger-spinners or wrist-spinners, might want to experiment with Ashley Mallet's low-tech method of practising flighted spin: a length of string hung across the net at a particular height, with the bowler then trying to get the ball to 'drop' over the string.

a: Underspin
b: Side-spin
c: Overspin

FIGURE 18: *Trajectories and directions that spin bowling can take. Note that all deliveries start above the batter's eyeline. The skill – especially with overspin and side-spin deliveries – is to keep the ball above the eyeline for as long as possible.*

THE DELIVERIES

Spinners are classified according to how the ball leaves the hand, which hand they use, whether they use their wrists or fingers to impart spin on the ball, and in which direction the ball turns. These are discussed in considerably more detail shortly, but a brief 'family tree' may be useful in order to fully understand the different breeds of spinners, and their various skills.

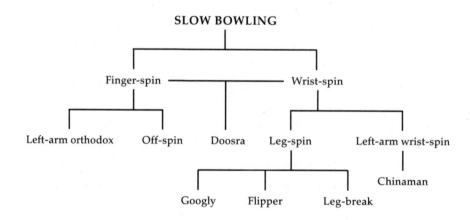

FIGURE 19: *The spinner's family tree*

What these various skills entail is dependent on which 'subspecies' the spinner belongs to, or rather on which side of the family tree he find himself (see Figure 19 on the facing page).

But most crucial to all spinners are spin and accuracy, and, as explained in the introduction, all control (whether it involves the line and length of seam bowling or the sharp lateral movement of spin) comes from a sound grip, a good release, and above all, a good action.

Thus it is vital to familiarize yourself with the grips and bowling actions of the two main 'subspecies' – wrist-spin and finger-spin – before we progress to a more general discussion of slow bowling.

For the sake of clarity we have separated these two types of bowler, but always remember that the principles of spin – turn, control, patience and cunning – apply to all slow bowlers, regardless of their specialty.

FINGER-SPIN

Somewhat less demanding than wrist-spin, finger-spin represents the natural first step for young bowlers looking to get the ball to deviate. Spin is imparted by a hard flick of the wrist and a quick tweaking of the fingers, as if the bowler were turning a doorknob violently or screwing off the top of a jar; while accuracy comes from a classical side-on action, the arm coming over more or less as it would with a seamer bowling a cutter or slower ball.

WRIST, THEN FINGERS

Although we carefully distinguish between finger-spin and wrist-spin, it should be noted that these are not strictly accurate descriptions. Both varieties of bowling use both fingers and wrist: the difference lies in which is used first. Finger-spin starts in the wrist and ends in the fingertips, while wrist-spin starts in the fingers and ends in the wrist.

The grip

The best way to illustrate the grip for the orthodox finger-spinner (whether right-arm off-spin or left-arm orthodox) is to demonstrate how to insert the ball into your fingers.

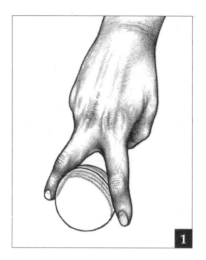 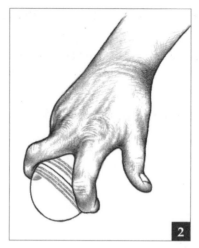 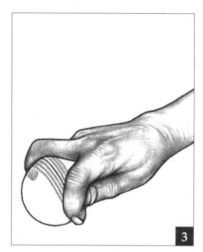

Spread the first and second fingers onto the seam of the ball, ensuring that the main pressure is exerted on the first finger (1). Now fold the hands down behind the ball, bending the fingers (2 and 3).

A useful variation on the orthodox finger-spun delivery is the 'floater', which is intended to beat the other edge of the bat.

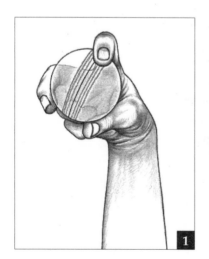 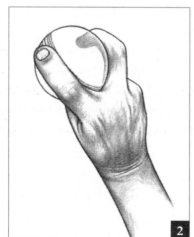 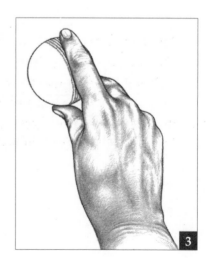

If you're playing between showers of rain or on a soggy outfield, and the ball has become wet and slippery, it can be extremely difficult to bowl off-spin as the ball tends to slip out of your fingers like a bar of soap. The solution is to narrow your grip slightly by drawing the fingers a little closer together. Now instead of spinning the ball with your fingers, use only the wrist.

Use the standard spread-fingers grip to deceive the batsman, but instead hold the ball so that the forefinger runs down the seam. The thumb adapts a sidewise position (as for an outswinger – see p. 57). As the ball is delivered, it comes off the ends of the fingers and floats away from the batsman, who may be expecting turn. This opens up the opportunity to get him caught behind or at slip, or even stumped if he walks past the ball. The left-arm orthodox spinner who is turning the ball away from the bat might use the floater to trap the batsman who is playing for turn LBW.

The action

If you were asked to put a marble or ball-bearing on a smooth table and to impart as much spin on it as you could, so that it would whirl around its vertical axis like a top for as long as possible, what would you do? The resulting actions on the little ball would be anything but gentle – no light flicking of the fingers over the edges of the sphere. On the contrary, you would grip it fairly hard, almost pinching it between forefinger and thumb, and then flick it out off the end of your thumb, for an instant pushing down on the sphere and the table as your fingers and hand lifted off and allowed it to spin.

The forces at work in this little exercise are emphatically not gentle. When you grip the sphere prior to spinning it, your fingers are squeezing in from opposite sides, both pushing it down into the table, and at the moment of release, it is pushed either against your thumb or forefinger, depending on how you chose to spin it.

All of which illustrates that spin is about resistance. The cricket ball is not a ball-bearing spinning unhindered in a cushion of oil, or even a wheel spinning on its horizontal axis around an axle. To impart 'rip' on the ball in cricket, you need to grip it, pinch it, squeeze it and tear at it. And that's just your fingers….

During your run-up or early in your action, cock your wrist in towards your body (1). As you release the ball, visualize opening a doorknob in the direction of the spin, and flick out your first finger, imparting downwards 'rip' on the ball (2 and 3).

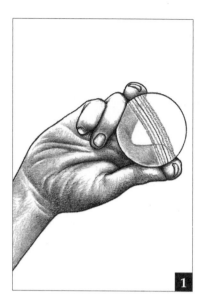 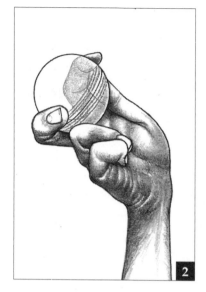 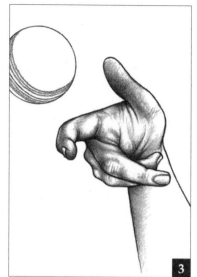

But the spin-generating friction or resistance of your finger dragging down the side of the ball is only half of the picture. When a whip cracks, it is the very tip of the whip that has flicked back on itself to create the sound we hear, but that speed and momentum had to be generated by a flick of the entire whip. In fact, without the fairly slow, leisurely movement in the first few feet of the whip, the 'business end' of the whip would go nowhere at all.

The same applies to finger-spin. If you stood side-on to a batsman with your feet rooted in place and your upper body immobile, and gave the ball the biggest rip you could muster with both fingers and wrist, you would see almost no deviation off the pitch. It might move away off the straight fractionally, but certainly there would be no bounce or 'fizz' off the wicket. Most tellingly, it would bounce slowly and predictably, allowing the batsman to pick his spot.

The reason for this is that spinners, and especially finger-spinners, gain a great deal of momentum and spin from the final pivot of their bodies around their front

All finger-spinners should work as hard as they can at strengthening their fingers, particularly their first and second fingers. This can be done in various ways, but the easiest and often most effective is either to click or snap the fingers very hard, or to screw the ball into the bowling hand with as much resistance as you can muster, as if polishing an apple, spreading the fingers and twisting the wrist around after the fingers.

foot. This has already been discussed in the section on the bowler's run-up, but it is worth repeating: the slow bowler's front foot must land and grip, providing traction around which his body can pivot.

If spinners take one piece of advice from this book, other than that they should aspire to putting revs on the ball, it is this: bowl the ball against your front foot, not around or over it.

Bowling as you land – letting the ball go while still on tiptoe – will produce almost no spin.

Likewise, we have already described the problem seen in many left-arm finger-spinners (left-arm orthodox): positioning their front foot incorrectly and then having to bowl around it, thereby ruining their angle of attack.

The off-break or slow left-arm orthodox action is fluid and rhythmical, but the young bowler should not confuse its fluidity or rhythm with the action of the fast bowler. The fast bowler's run-up and delivery can be broken down into unique actions, but they flow together to form an almost uninterrupted whole. The mistake young spinners can make is to emulate this smooth action, with the result that they bowl as they land.

Instead they need to understand that the pivot – that vital gripping and grinding of the spikes into the bowling crease – is what produces spin, and that it essentially acts as an interruption of the bowling action.

In other words, the finger-spinner's action might be broken down in the following way – identical to the standard seam delivery, except for that one crucial interruption:

Bowl the ball against your front foot, not around or over it.

| Run-up; | Gather; | Set-up; | Unfold; | PIVOT; | Delivery; | Follow-through. |

© QUINTIC

The panel above illustrates the classic off-spinner's action:
- a pronounced sideways turn in the gather, so that the shoulders and chest are perpendicular to the bowling crease
- superb external rotation of the shoulder
- a high arm, just off '12 o'clock'
- the right knee kicking through with the rotation of the trunk, wrenching the front foot round into its pivot to create spin
- a complete follow-through.

VERTICAL DISCUS VERSUS JAVELIN

Just as young fast bowlers are usually urged to learn the 'classic' side-on action, so finger-spinners, whether right- or left-handed, have also traditionally been encouraged to look over their leading shoulder at the target. For over a century, off-spinners have wheeled in, side-on and tall, reaching for the sky with their leading arm before cartwheeling over with high actions and exaggerated pivots on their front foot, as demonstrated in the photographs below.

This shows the orthodox action, with the head dropping away slightly as the shoulder and rigid arm wheel past, a movement reminiscent of a discus thrower, albeit one tilted over towards the vertical.

And then came Muralitharan….

As illustrated above, the Sri Lankan bowls almost entirely chest-on to the batsman, with the result that instead of delivering with the 'vertical discus' action, he almost spears the ball in from above his shoulder, like a javelin thrower. The debate surrounding his highly unorthodox action is discussed in more detail in the section on throwing on pp. 22–37, but we believe that Muralitharan is the first of many bowlers who will use this front-on method of delivery, their ultra-flexible wrists (and elbows) extracting much greater turn and accuracy than the traditional action.

HIGH ARM VERSUS ROUND ARM

We have emphasized that spin is generated by the body swivelling against the front foot (first against the traction provided by the spikes under the ball of the foot, then against the foot as a whole, pressing down heel and toe into the pitch).

But of course it is not your front foot that makes the ball spin, nor even the strong rotation of your shoulders: many fast bowlers have a particularly quick and strong pivot, and they don't spin the ball through the air. Instead it is your arm, combining with the 'whip-crack' of the wrist and hands, which imparts turn.

So why is the body pivot important at all? The answer is a matter of simple biomechanics: the off-spinner flicks his fingers down the side of the ball as he squeezes it out of his hand, but this action would be fairly ineffective without a full downward sweep of the bowling arm, cutting across his body as he follows through.

It makes sense, therefore, that the angle of the arm would have to be that best suited to slicing down the side of the ball and cutting across the body. You don't need to be a spin bowler of any experience to feel that this angle is one just offset from the vertical. Try to slice down next to or under the ball held at '12 o'clock', and you'll drag it straight down, or have to rotate your wrist under it at some point. This is why seamers try to keep their arm vertical, since it is much easier to impart power and pace into a ball by bringing the hand down onto it from directly above.

In other words, the spinner needs to vary the position of his arm from between '10 o'clock' and 'high noon' to change the amount spin he puts on the ball.

Interestingly, almost all the great finger-spinners have had reasonably 'low' arms, coming through at around '11 o'clock'. In addition to an almost round-arm action, these bowlers also kept a slight kink in their elbows: instead of locking the elbow as a fast bowler would, they maintained a slight angle, bowling with a fractionally bent arm that allowed them get beside and under the ball more easily. This also allowed the shoulder muscles to become more involved in imparting spin and force on the ball.

A lower arm action gives you two levers instead of one: first the shoulder, then the wrist.

Remember, there is nothing in the Laws of cricket that says you may not bowl with a bent arm: it is straightening the arm during the delivery that is illegal. Paul Adams (although not a finger-spinner) kept his bowling arm flexed at almost 20° throughout its arc.

The 'classic' action of Saqlain Mushtaq on p. 97 illustrates a standard high action, one that should be encouraged in young bowlers; but even here the arm is coming through at about 'half past eleven'. More experienced bowlers, trying to extract more spin (perhaps bowling in favourable conditions or with a good lead), tend to drop the arm, as illustrated here by the great English finger-spinner Jim Laker.

© QUINTIC

Many modern coaches insist on the more upright 'classic' action, but Laker was able to get prodigious turn, as well as flight and accuracy, from a flatter action. Another considerable benefit of a lower arm position is that it enables you to bowl the under-cutter, a favourite of Laker and Ray Illingworth. It is delivered with an even lower arm than illustrated here, which makes the ball drift away towards the off side.

To sum up, while elements of the finger-spinner's action are sacrosanct, there is room for experimentation with both the position of the body at delivery (side-on or front-on), and the angle of the arm. Try and find what feels most comfortable and is effective for you.

THE AERODYNAMICS OF SPIN AND THE MAGNUS EFFECT

Although warfare in the late-eighteenth and early-nineteenth centuries was bloodier than anything the world had known until then, with massive amounts of firepower discharged over short distances at densely packed armies of men, a remarkably small number of musket-balls and bullets fired actually hit their targets.

Indeed, in his book *Acts of War* (2003), military historian Richard Holmes describes a kind of combat in which kills seemed almost miraculous:

> *The Comte de Guibert, in this respect the most optimistic of the theorists of the horse and musket age, thought that one million rounds of musketry produced 2 000 casualties: one hit, that is, for every 500 rounds… Major-General B.P. Hughes, a modern authority, argues: 'It is impossible to accept that more than about 5% of the bullets that could have been fired were effective, and the rate often seems to have been appreciably lower' (2003, p. 167).*

There were various reasons for this extremely low kill rate: many soldiers threw thrift and discipline to the wind, blindly discharging their muskets in the general direction of the foe, regardless of range. Most were dealing with unpredictable and temperamental weapons. But it was also a simple matter of physics: most shots fired with good aim and within range simply drifted off their intended line, swinging away to the left or right of the target, or swooping up over his head.

It was a phenomenon that troubled generals and their political masters, locked as they were in an expensive arms race in a European continent beset by violent squabbles between nations, each kingdom or empire working frantically to get a technological edge over its enemies.

Not surprisingly, most army leaders had turned not only to engineers, but to scientists and physicists, and a German professor called Heinrich Magnus was duly commissioned by the Prussian Army to study the trajectory of artillery shells. The phenomenon he saw – rotating artillery shells deflecting in the direction opposite to that of their spin – was nothing new to most gunners or marksmen of the eighteenth and early-nineteenth centuries, but it was the German who explained the phenomenon, publishing his findings in 1852, and (unfortunately) accelerating the development of the rifle-barrels of modern firearms.

What frustrated nineteenth-century generals is an entirely familiar sight to modern sports fans. Whether it's Shane Warne's leg-break, a top-spin shot by Roger Federer, a free kick by David Beckham, or Johnny Wilkinson's touch-finder, the Magnus effect features in almost every ball sport, sending balls of all shapes and sizes deflecting in the direction opposite to that of their spin, whether around a vertical, horizontal or diagonal axis. (Of course, amateur golfers might call it something less scientific and more explicit when it sends their sliced drives swinging away into the long grass!)

More than a century after Magnus's first observations, scientist Lyman Briggs (1959) used the Magnus effect to explain why a rapidly spinning (seamed) baseball or a smooth ball without seams both curve in their flight (although the direction of the curve may be different for seamed and seamless balls).

The explanation for the Magnus effect involves the simple principle discussed earlier; air travelling more rapidly over one side of a sphere will produce an area of low pressure on that side. This area of low pressure will then cause the ball to deviate in its direction.

FIGURE 20: *The aerodynamics of the Magnus effect*

Figure 20 shows the air flow patterns around a delivery moving towards the top of the page; the delivery is spinning counter-clockwise in the vertical axis. This delivery is almost impossible to bowl (Clarrie Grimmett may have managed this with his round-arm action, and Warne did so every so often when aiming for a flipper), except for a right-arm wrist-spinner with a very low action, in which he releases the ball from the right side of his hand with his palm horizontal and pointing towards the ground. A left-arm wrist-spinner might also be able to bowl this ball by releasing it slightly later than he would his googly, i.e., with his palm facing up. However, it most clearly illustrates the principles involved here.

If the contortions and reversed hand positions of leg-spin bowling are confusing, try picturing instead a David Beckham free kick, in which his foot strikes the ball with his right foot on its right side. The spin on the ball is therefore counter-clockwise around its vertical axis, which will cause the ball to swerve to the left late in its flight.

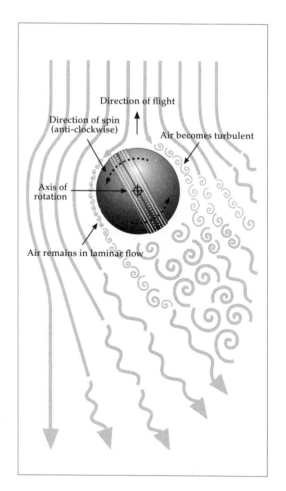

The Magnus effect occurs because the edge of the ball that is turning into the oncoming wind 'trips' the boundary layer, producing turbulent flow in the boundary layer on that side of the ball, the right side in Figure 20 (Mehta, 1985). In contrast, laminar flow of high speed occurs on the surface spinning in the same direction as the air travelling over that surface, the left side of Figure 20. In contrast to what occurs in the case in the swinging delivery (see Figure 16 in the section on the physics of swing), the laminar flow separates from the surface of the ball later than the turbulent flow on the right-hand side of the delivery does. This is because the turbulence is generated by the vigorous spinning of the ball into the face of the on-rushing air (whereas the turbulent flow produced by the seam in the swinging delivery shown in Figure 16 occurs across a surface that is spinning backwards, i.e., in the direction of travel – not at 90° to that direction).

As a result, a horizontal force develops towards the left, which pushes the ball laterally through the air in what we would see as 'drift'. Interestingly, the nature of the ball's surface influences the magnitude of the Magnus effect, which is much greater in a fluffy new tennis ball than in a smooth ball – like a cricket ball. This is because the fluffy surface of the tennis ball produces a greater disturbance of flow on the side advancing into the on-rushing air, producing an earlier separation point and hence a greater pressure difference across the ball.

Figure 21 shows what is effectively the top-spinner (or a fairly straight doosra) bowled by a leg-spinner or off-spinner: the axis of the spin in Figure 20 opposite has been rotated 90° to the left so that the ball is spinning forwards in the horizontal plane directly towards the batsman, who would be on the left side of the page. The delivery is being viewed from the side – i.e., from the off side (mid-off or cover) – of a ball moving towards the left of the page. In this case, the direction of drift is directly downwards, resulting in the delivery 'dipping' or 'dropping' on the batsman, pitching shorter than he would have expected. This delivery will also bounce more steeply.

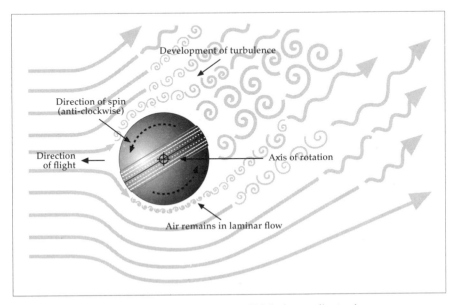

FIGURE 21: *The aerodynamics of the top-spinner – which is about to dip steeply*

And if the axis of ball spin is rotated a further 90° to the left, so that the axis of spin runs horizontally through the ball pointing towards the batsman, no drift will occur, as the axis of spin is now in the same plane as the direction of travel – so the effects of the rotation are the same on both sides of the ball (see Figure 22). Depending on the direction in which the ball is spinning, the delivery would be either a maximal spinning leg- or off-spin delivery that will turn maximally, but will not drift.

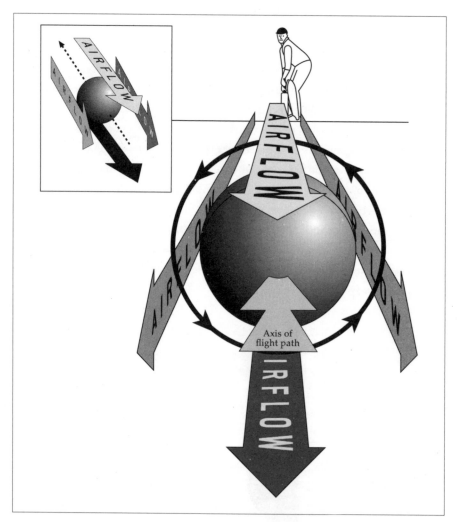

FIGURE 22: *Leg- or off-spin delivery in which no drift will occur, as the axis of spin is now in the same plane as the direction of travel*

However, if the axis of spin is angled slightly to the angle of travel, then the Magnus effect occurs and becomes maximal when the angle of spin is at 90° to the direction in which the ball is travelling.

THE MAGNUS EFFECT AND
'THE BALL OF THE CENTURY'

Probably the most famous ball ever sent down in Test cricket was Shane Warne's first delivery in an Ashes Test match. Also referred to as the 'Ball From Hell', the 'Gatting Ball', or simply 'That Ball', it was delivered shortly after 3pm on 4 June 1993 at Old Trafford cricket ground. England looked well set, and the experienced Mike Gatting anticipated no problems facing a green young spinner.

The leg-break Warne bowled to Gatting drifted towards leg, dipping late in its trajectory. The batsman's sensible response was to plant his leg, bat alongside, towards the pitch of the ball – which proved to be the wrong line. The ball pitched outside the leg stump, before spinning back fiercely past the edge of the bat to clip the top of the off-stump. The expression on Gatting's face when he realized his bails had been scattered is one of the classic images of modern cricket. (A similar delivery bowled to South African Herschelle Gibbs in the famous tied 1999 World Cup semi-final was possibly the single most important factor in determining that Australia advanced to the final in that case – last-minute run-outs notwithstanding!)

What happened from an aerodynamic point of view? Generally, a ball moving away from us in the horizontal plane, and spinning from right to left (anti-clockwise) moves to the left (equivalent to the off side in cricket) and not to the right (leg side). This can be seen when a right-sided kicker in football takes a penalty and strikes the ball on its right side (as in Figure 20). The ball always curves to the left. But in this case, Shane Warne spun the ball from right to left – yet it deviated to the right (leg side). Had it deviated to the left (as expected), Gatting would have been in line to play an appropriate shot.

In order for the delivery to drift towards leg, the wake of the ball must be disturbed upwards towards the off side. How this happens is not yet well described in the scientific literature. Thus, some speculation is warranted – and illustrated in Figure 23 overleaf.

If the axis of rotation of the delivery is in the same direction as the direction of the forward movement of the delivery, then the delivery will not drift (as shown in Figure 22). Thus to bowl his 'Ball from Hell', Warne had to have the axis of rotation of the delivery at an angle to its direction

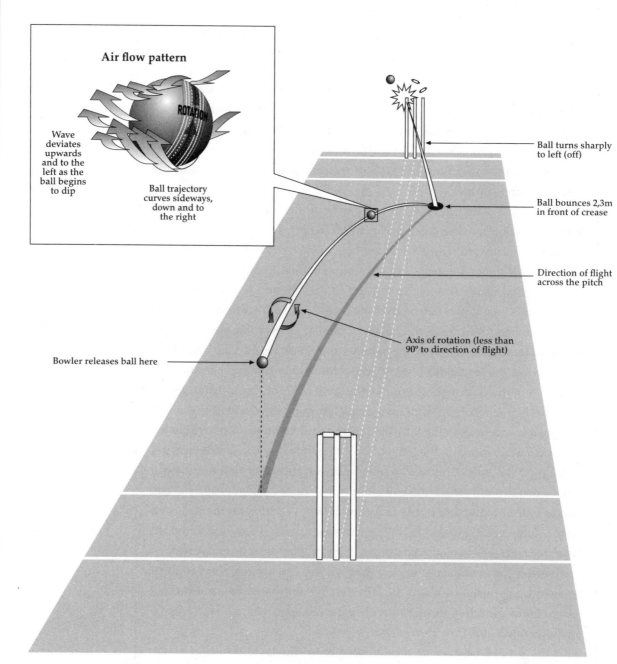

Air flow pattern

Wave deviates upwards and to the left as the ball begins to dip

ROTATION

Ball trajectory curves sideways, down and to the right

Ball turns sharply to left (off)

Ball bounces 2,3m in front of crease

Direction of flight across the pitch

Axis of rotation (less than 90° to direction of flight)

Bowler releases ball here

FIGURE 23: *The probable aerodynamic effects that produced the 'Ball of the Century'*

of movement. Most likely, the seam was tilted slightly backwards from the vertical (when seen from above), with the seam on the left side of the ball slightly ahead. In this position, the axis of rotation (seen from behind the ball) is upwards and to the leg side (see Figure 23).

For this delivery to drift downwards and to the leg, when viewed from behind, the wake must be disturbed upwards and to the off side. This requires that the air on the leg side and the bottom of the ball must travel faster around the back of the ball than the air travelling on the off side and the top of the ball. This would be explained by the Magnus effect, since the leading edge and top surface of the ball is turning into the onrushing air (towards the off side), whereas the air on the bottom and the leg side of the ball is travelling in the same direction as the spin on the ball. As a result, the air on the leg side and bottom of the ball travels more rapidly, producing the area of low pressure into which the ball drifts and drops.

The challenge for Warne in delivering That Ball was to ensure that the axis of rotation on his delivery was not so far towards the leg side that the Magnus effect would produce purely a downward force (as demonstrated in Figure 21 on p. 103); but was also not in the direction of the ball's flight, in which case there would be neither drift nor drop even though the amount of turn would likely be maximal. But this axis of rotation also had to be optimal to produce the degree of turn necessary to beat Gatting's legs, body and bat.

Finally, Warne had to put enough revolutions on the ball to ensure that there was a meaningful difference in the speed of the air moving over the advancing and retreating surfaces of his delivery so that the Magnus effect would indeed be achieved – and so that the ball would turn enough to get past Gatting's defences.

If we are correct in our speculations, and Figure 23 correctly illustrates the physics of what occurred that afternoon, then this ball is no longer one of 'mystery'. However, what is in absolutely no doubt is the exceptional degree of technical mastery required to bowl it – as a delivery it truly deserves its monikers 'Ball of the Century' and 'Ball in a Million'. It is little wonder that many consider Warne to be the greatest leg-spin bowler in the history of the game – for more on this, see pp. 116–18.

WRIST-SPIN

A wrist-spinner is a rare breed, possessing a skill that takes years of hard graft and devotion to master. If seam bowling and finger-spin are akin to throwing the ball conventionally (by letting it leave the fingers in the direction desired), then wrist-spin is about trying to land the ball on a small target 18 metres away by effectively losing control of the throw, with the ball slipping out of the side or the back of the hand at the moment of release. Not surprisingly, the thoroughbred leg-spinner is a once-a-generation phenomenon. But even for those wrist-spinners not blessed with the skills (or downright genius) of a Shane Warne or Abdul Qadir, landing a hard-spun 'leggie' on a good length and watching the ball fizz past the bat is surely one of cricket's greatest pleasures.

Accuracy will always be a challenge to young wrist-spinners, but once mastered, the fourfold value of wrist-spin becomes clear:

- **The stock ball of the right-hander turns away from the right-handed batsman.** It is more difficult to make late adjustments to a ball turning away from the body than into it.
- **It allows for the googly and top-spinner,** whereas the conventional finger-spinner can only use the top-spinner or floater as variations.
- **It generates considerably more spin than finger-spin.**
- **It opens up a target area on the pitch that forms the end of the run-up of right-arm fast bowlers bowling over the wicket.** Rough outside the right-hander's leg-stump can be fatal (M. Gatting, b. S. Warne, 1993), while rough outside a left-hander's off-stump can be just as fraught (A. Strauss, b. S. Warne, 2005).

LEG-SPIN

'Leg-spin' or the leg-break delivery has traditionally described the ball that pitches and 'breaks' or spins from the leg side to the off side, just as off-spin or the off-break delivery 'breaks' from the off to the leg. However, left-handed wrist-spinners also qualify as 'leg-spinners' by virtue of having an identical action to right-handers. The left-hander's 'leg-break' is known as the chinaman, and naturally spins into the right-hander. For the sake of clarity and brevity, we will use the term 'leg-spin' and 'leg-spinner' for both right- and left-handed bowlers, to underline the fact that these two 'separate' varieties of bowler are simply mirror images of one another, both letting go of the ball out of the side of the hand with a big rotation of the wrist.

The young leg-spinner is faced with a task considerably more daunting than that of the young off-spinner, who has his thumb and index finger to help him

'Keep it simple: develop a hard-spun leg-break which you can bowl on a perfect length, and make that your stock ball.'

– Richie Benaud

LEFT-ARM SPINNERS: A RARE BREED

Since left-handers comprise just 10% of the global population, it is not surprising that so few left-arm leg-spinners have risen through the ranks of Test cricket. South Africa's Paul Adams enjoyed a meteoric rise in international cricket, many batsmen finding his contorted action extremely difficult to separate from his more conventional flight and turn; but Adams' star waned as accuracy problems, and an easily identifiable 'wrong'un', made him increasingly vulnerable to attack. Australia's selectors also experimented with Michael Bevan and Brad Hogg: Bevan even enjoyed an extremely brief billing as a Test all-rounder, while Hogg had considerable success in the 2007 World Cup with his conventional chinaman delivery and exceptional accuracy.

guide the ball. This means he needs to keep it simple, and to learn to bowl the basic delivery required by his discipline. For Richie Benaud, the greatest leg-spinner of his generation, this basic delivery was uncomplicated, and he explained it to Shane Warne as follows: 'Keep it simple: develop a hard-spun leg-break which you can bowl on a perfect length, and make that your stock ball.'

It wasn't a revolutionary idea, insisted Benaud, attributing it to Clarrie Grimmett, who preceded him in the Australian halls of leg-spinner fame, and pointing out that it had been his own father's basic philosophy and advice. Being able to bowl the big turning leggie at will and landing it more or less where you intended has two purposes, explains Benaud:

> *First, the bowler is able to take wickets with it and secondly, just as important, if anyone is threatening to hand him a belting, he is able to fall back on it as a defensive measure* (1998, p. 210).

Of course leg-spin bowling wouldn't be half the craft and spectacle it is without all the variations it contains – googlies, flippers, top-spinners and so on – but before we discuss these, it is important to get to grips with the delivery itself and the action it requires.

The grip

The grip for the leg-break, as bowled by a right-arm wrist-spinner. (Left-handed bowlers can simply reverse this.)

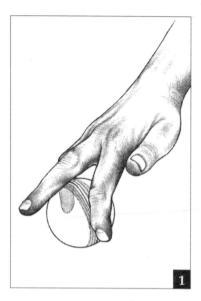  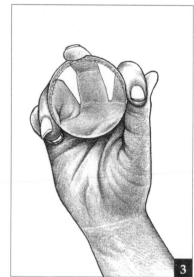

The grip for wrist-spinning does not rely on the pressure points of the fingers as much as orthodox spinning, but relies on a very supple wrist. The grip starts with the first and third fingers running down the seam of the ball, with the second finger resting on top (1). Fold the hand down behind the ball until the thumb is running parallel to the seam (2 and 3).

The action

Cock the wrist down and away from the body (1). As the arm swings over in the bowling action, the wrist flicks open as if you are opening a door anti-clockwise (2 and 3). It is important to keep the bowling arm very high when delivering the ball: this will create the natural in-drift and dip that can be enhanced even more if bowling into the wind. As the bowling arm comes over, the front leg should be braced. The back leg will pivot around it, turning the shoulder towards the batsman.

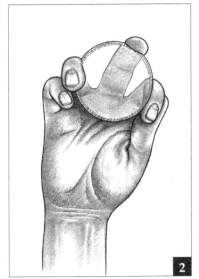

The googly

As stated earlier, the spinner deceives his prey by confusing him about one or more of the following aspects of the delivery:

*   **where it will pitch**
*   **when it will pitch**
*   **where it will go after pitching.**

'Picking' the direction of the spin is something batsmen work very hard at, either by watching the bowler's action and hand, or by watching the ball through the air, so that they don't have to adopt the last-ditch tactic of 'reading the spin off the wicket' – a rather charitable way of describing a desperate attempt to adapt one's shot after seeing which way the ball has spun.

It therefore poses severe problems to the batsman when a particular action (which he has become accustomed to watching, and which always sends the ball in a certain direction) suddenly produces a delivery that goes in the opposite direction. The doubt created in his mind is as valuable as extreme pace or a proud seam: suddenly his early-warning radar – his view of the action and hand – has been 'jammed'.

Which was exactly what B.J.T. Bosanquet realized when, on a tour of Australia in 1903/04 with the MCC, he bowled a ball with a leg-break action that spun like an off-break. The googly had been born. However, it was another seven years before the delivery gained wider recognition. Albert Vogler and Reg Schwarz, the South African slow bowlers who perfected the delivery, have been largely forgotten by popular cricket lore, but the discomfort to which they subjected the Australians of the 1910/11 tour made it clear that the delivery had arrived to stay (Schwarz, who had studied Bosanquet's methods and who bowled only googlies, took 59 Australian wickets). Today, the variety of names by which it is known is an illustration of how deeply it has entrenched itself into the lore of the game: whether you know it as the 'wrong'un' (because it turns the 'wrong way'), the 'other one', the 'google', or, in Afrikaans, the 'gool-bal', it is a vital and potentially lucrative skill to have as a leg-spinner.

Most great 'leggies' have possessed a decent googly, but some made it their trump card. Abdul Qadir's 'other one' was not only beautifully disguised, but turned an unusually long way. South African Denys Hobson possessed a vicious googly, but his country's politics robbed him of the chance to bamboozle batsmen in the international arena, and he spent his playing days lobbing fizzing leg-breaks and googlies into the howling summer south-easter at Newlands in Cape Town, gaining phenomenal dip and in-drift.

The grip and action

The back of the hand (instead of the ball) faces the batsman at the moment of delivery. Because of the position of the seam as the ball leaves the hand, it turns in towards the batsman with a similar action to the leg-spinner. Since the arm comes over very quickly, even when bowling spin, it can be very difficult for the batsman to pick which way the ball is going to turn. An incorrect observation, a poor choice of shot – and it's all over.

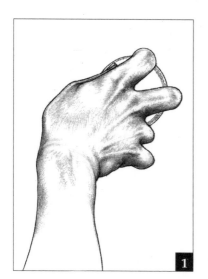 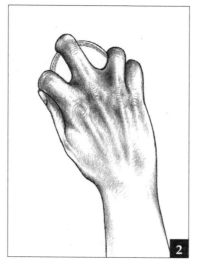 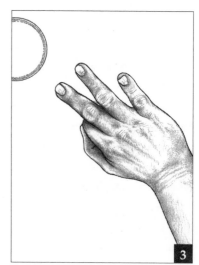

The googly needs a much higher arm than the leg-break, which is best spun with more of a round-arm action. Warne spun his leg-breaks a long way with his arm held lower, but he always struggled to bowl a particularly good googly for the same reason. On the other hand, a bowler like Mushtaq Ahmed, whose googlies could turn as much as his leg-breaks, came over with an almost vertical arm, his head dropping away to allow the arm and shoulder to come over. India's Anil Kumble is another good example of a leg-spinner with a good googly; his high arm reduced the amount of spin he got on the leg-break, but enabled the googly to nip back appreciably.

Peter Philpott, author of the definitive book on wrist-spin bowling, notes that for those starting to practise the googly, it might help to drop the left shoulder (for right-handed bowlers) and open the body. However, he feels that as the bowler gains confidence, and if the wrist, fingers, forearm, elbow and shoulder are doing their job, the action should be no different to that for the leg-break – otherwise the bowler will reveal the delivery to the batsman and lose the element of surprise.

A WARNING TO YOUNG LEG-SPINNERS AND COACHES

A common problem when a youngster starts practising the googly is that his wrist does not return to the basic wrist-spin position, and he loses the ability to bowl the conventional leg-break.

Peter Philpott advises, 'Don't bowl all wrong'uns [googlies] for a week or even a few days.' He prefers his charges to bowl a sequence of different deliveries. He also suggests practising the googly underarm until it has been completely mastered; then moving to roundarm, and then only to overarm. This way the bowler can watch his fingers and wrist in action.

The skill of wrist-spinning is the toughest of all. For any player wishing to master this skill, there has to be a massive commitment to practise.

The flipper

There are two types of flipper: the underhand flipper and side flipper. As demonstrated by Warne in the early stages of his career, the flipper is deadly because it looks as if it's been dropped short, which invites the batsman to rock back to pull it. In fact it is short, but the over-spin on it – or the lack of any spin – means that it doesn't bounce and sit up to be hit, but instead skids onto the batsman, easily trapping him LBW.

The other lethal aspect of the flipper is that it doesn't 'break' to the off side, instead coming on dead straight. This has been the undoing of numerous batsmen who played forward along a leg-break line (allowing for some turn), only to have the ball hold its line and skid past the inside edge of the bat into the pads or stumps. Because it doesn't bounce, if it hits the pads, it is almost invariably inches off the ground, so even if the batsman gets a stride in, he's in serious danger of being given out LBW.

According to Richie Benaud, the flipper is bowled from beneath the wrist. It is squeezed out the fingers so that it spins around its own axis as it travels down the pitch. Benaud warns, 'It should never be used by young bowlers until their ligaments, tendons and muscles are strong enough. It puts far too great a strain on young bodies' (*MCC Masterclass*, 1994, p. 56).

VARIATIONS AND MYSTERY BALLS

Great spinners invent new deliveries every so often – or at least rediscover neglected ones, and rebrand them as something new and terrifying! Shane Warne's 'flipper' was the bane of the cricketing world in the early 1990s, despite it having been invented at least 70 years earlier and used by Clarrie Grimmett. When injury forced him to retire the delivery, he kept working, eventually producing the slider, the 'zooter' and various other unnamed deliveries that may or may not have been 'new' to the game.

Be careful, however, to back up the hype with some sort of potency. South African pundits were all ears when very occasional off-spinner Mark Waugh alluded to his new 'knuckle-ball' on Australia's tour in 1996. The delivery lived up to its name, tossed out of the knuckles of an almost closed fist. Boland batsman Kenny Jackson treated the first one with curious respect, but the rest were given the treatment they deserved, and dispatched to all corners of the Paarl grounds. The knuckle-ball was instantly retired. Having said that, some variations and mystery balls have proved extremely effective.

THE DOOSRA

By 1996, the world's batsmen were quickly shaking themselves out into two categories: those who couldn't play Shane Warne, and those who couldn't play him yet. The Australian had revitalized slow bowling, and with Pakistani leg-spinner Mushtaq Ahmed mopping up everyone Warne hadn't, it seemed that the 'leggie' was the game's new super-predator.

Off-spinners, on the other hand, promised some respite. Difficult to get away, yes, but the traditional finger-spinner suddenly seemed something of a port in a storm of wrist-spin.

But all of that changed when a lanky young Pakistani off-spinner made the ball spin from leg to off. Batsmen could only watch in horror as Saqlain Mushtaq's flighted 'off-breaks' straightened into their pads or jagged away off the outside edge. The doosra had arrived.

The delivery was probably named by Pakistani wicket-keeper Moin Khan, exhorting Saqlain in Urdu to bowl 'the other one' – 'doosra' literally means 'the second one'. There is also some debate around whether or not Saqlain invented the ball, with some claiming the honour for West Indian great Sonny Ramadhin, who also made the ball turn both ways from a conventional off-break grip.

However, there is no disputing that it was Saqlain who first demonstrated the devastating power of the doosra to a global audience, and his dominance in one-day cricket in the 1990s underlines the value of the delivery.

Strictly speaking, the doosra is a weapon of the finger-spinner, but we have decided to include it in this discussion of wrist-spin largely because it behaves like a leg-break, and is delivered with much more wrist and elbow movement than finger action.

When used by masters like Muttiah Muralitharan, it is a complex and difficult delivery, but the simple theory behind the doosra is that it is an off-break with the wrist turned around so that the ball goes the other way, with the seam pointing at first slip instead of leg gully. When you bowl a conventional off-break, your palm and pulse are facing the bowler. When you bowl a doosra, it is your knuckles and the top of your wrist that face down the pitch. Put another way, if you are bowling wearing a watch (which you shouldn't be!), the off-break delivery should show the batsman your watch-strap, while the doosra should show him the time.

However, much of the controversy around the doosra stems from the fact that in order to impart spin, there needs to be some flexing of the elbow, which is why some bowlers have been forced to abandon the doosra altogether – or else water it down so dramatically that it becomes a pointless delivery.

The legalities will no doubt be thrashed out at some stage in the near future, but we feel that it is an exciting development in the game, and in view of the tremendous skill required to learn it – and bowl it on a length – we believe it should be allowed and encouraged.

Richie Benaud's advice to a young Warne was to perfect the hard-spun leg-break as his stock ball: 'I added that it would take him at least four years of extremely hard work to perfect it,' wrote Benaud in 1995. 'He did it in two.'

SHANE WARNE: THE BEST WRIST-SPINNER OF ALL TIME?

In 2000, an elite panel of judges selected five Wisden Cricketers of the Century, players whose spectacular career would represent the epitome of cricketing virtuosity for future generations. The men they chose were Sir Donald Bradman, Sir Jack Hobbs, Sir Garfield Sobers, Sir Vivian Richards, and Shane Warne. The fact that Warne was the only player in the group who has not been knighted for his services to cricket was somehow fitting for a player who, throughout his career, seemed as comfortable with his iconoclastic bad boy image as he was with the mantle of match-winner, mentor and class act.

The bowler responsible for the most famous delivery in Test cricket; the first spinner to reach 500 Test wickets; the first bowler of any kind to reach 600 and then 700; match-winner for four Australian captains; tormentor of England (and the nemesis of South Africa's gifted batsman Daryl Cullinan); Man of the Match in a World Cup final; a self-taught expert in psychological warfare and marketing – Warne riveted and enraged, enthralled and astounded from the first moment he came to the cricketing world's attention.

But the greatest slow bowler of his generation – and perhaps of any generation – had his critics. After all, as well as the illustrious list of accomplishments above, he was sent home from a World Cup series for taking diet pills and thus failing a drug test – and then there was his knack for having his sexual peccadilloes splashed across the tabloids.

Whether it was his love-life, his smoking, his weight, his form, his inability to bowl a good googly, the state of his bowling shoulder, or a one-year ban for taking a banned diuretic, the nay-sayers were never short of a word. If they were to be believed, Warne was past it and a has-been by 1998, then by 1999, then by 2002. By the time the immortal Ashes series of 2005 began, with Warne two months shy of his 36th birthday, there was talk of it being his last series. By the summer's end, he had claimed 40 English wickets, the most in an Ashes Test series since Jim Laker took 46 in 1956, and the fourth most in a five-Test series in the history of cricket.

Halfway through his fifth Test, way back in 1992, things were looking less rosy: a career total of 5 wickets for 451 threatened to end his career before it had begun, and his captain Allan Border's faith must have been wavering. But then came the second innings against the West Indies in that Boxing Day Test, with a haul of 7 for 52, and the rest is a phenomenal history.

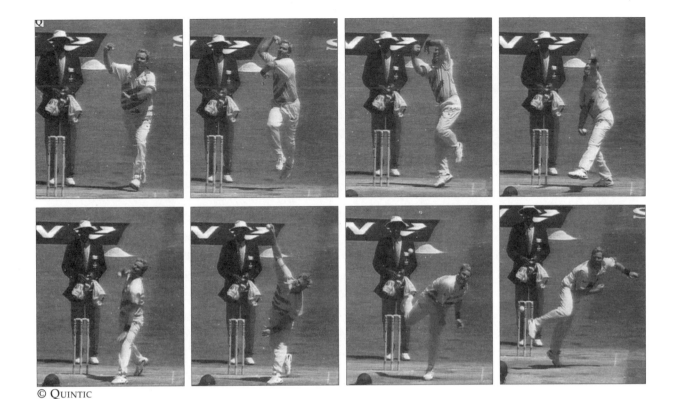

© QUINTIC

WHAT MADE HIM THE GREATEST?

According to Richie Benaud, it was Warne's brain and character as much as his bowling hand that accounted for his success:

> He has the ability, the nerve and the desire. That's close to an ideal combination but not quite all that is needed. You need an enquiring mind, an ability to sift good information from mediocre – and a genuine liking of hard work. The hard work is essential because the first requirement of those odd people who bowl out of the back of the hand is that they must develop that hard-spun stock ball.
>
> Show me someone who just rolls it out of his fingers and bowls accurately, and you can almost guarantee a steady bowler of county or Sheffield Shield standard. But show me someone who spins it hard, with over-spin as well as side-spin, and then develops accuracy through sheer hard work – and you have a young bowler with a real chance.
>
> The other vitally important aspect is that he had the complete confidence of his captain (1998, p. 213).

The brilliance of Warne's action: an extended front arm that doesn't go across his body but instead pulls down in front and to the leg side of his front leg; a superb head position, and a strong, aggressive follow-through.

Or, as was the case, captains: Allan Border had complete faith in his young find, but it was Mark Taylor who gave Warne the licence to attack, inventing the so-called 'Star Wars' field for the spinner, so named because it resembled the claustrophobic channels of the Death Star through which Luke Skywalker has to fly in the climactic sequence of that film, attacked on all sides by fighters and anti-aircraft artillery. In the cricketing version, there are at least two men around the bat in front of the wicket, a slip and gully, and sometimes a leg slip.

Something else worth mentioning is the quality of the relationship Warne had with his keepers, in particular Ian Healy. Healy combined superb keeping skills with a personal style that was immensely supportive of Warne, at the same time as extremely aggressive towards to the unfortunate batsmen – who must often have felt stuck between a rock and a hard place. Healy's most intimidating habit was to swing the ball at the stumps every time he took it, constantly reminding the batsman that if he played forward, he risked a stumping.

To analyze the success of a superstar like the Australian is to perhaps strip away some of the lustre and mystery, but it is nonetheless worth doing. In our view, Warne's greatness could be attributed to the following factors:

- the ability to spin the ball a long way, and to control the degree of turn he got
- supreme accuracy
- variation, guile and drift
- a clean, superb technique
- big bounce due to his wrist action (as much bounce, if not more, than Anil Kumble)
- aggression (as aggressive as any 150km/h strike bowler)
- a very dramatic and plausible style of appealing
- belief in himself
- an easy-going persona off the field (he was popular with most of his teammates)
- excellent publicity ('I've invented a new delivery!')
- a terrific work ethic
- the ability and patience to analyze his opponent technically and mentally.

The antics and negative publicity of Warne's early career (not to mention the sleazier aspects of his private life that emerged later on) have prejudiced many parents against him as a role model for their cricketing children. But as a bowler, he remains the yardstick to which all youngsters eager to bowl spin should aspire.

AND THE LAST WORD GOES TO CLARRIE GRIMMETT

In bringing a book on the extraordinary and multi-faceted skill of bowling to an end, we considered the question of legacy – a subject very dear to Bob Woolmer's heart. Bob believed that part of the cricketing coach's duty was to pass on the wisdom learnt from mentors and peers. Australian former Test player, captain and coach Bobby Simpson also stressed the importance of peer influence in cricket, and its relevance to the remarkable success and international dominance of Australian cricket in the current era. Leg-spin bowling, of which Simpson was himself an exponent, is one discipline in which the importance of this peer influence is very clear. Beginning with Bill O'Reilly and Clarrie Grimmett, selected as the two wrist-spin bowlers in Bradman's Best cricket team of all time (Perry, 2001), and extending through Richie Benaud to Shane Warne, Australian leg-spinners have always been among the world's very best.

Benaud has said that he was introduced to the art of leg-spin bowling through the excellent writing of Clarrie Grimmett, the contemporary of Don Bradman; and this legacy of superb manuals on spin bowling has been continued by Peter Philpott, whose *The Art of Wrist-spin Bowling* Bob Woolmer considered one of the best cricket coaching books he had encountered. Fortunately, literature knows no national borders, and young spinners and their coaches don't need to be Australian to benefit from Philpott's book and others like it, enormously valuable compendiums containing a century of hard-earned knowledge and strategy about leg-spin bowling.

But if the writing of Philpott and Benaud have publicized and elaborated on the art of slow bowling, it was Grimmett who literally wrote the book on spin. What follows are selections from his classic texts, *Taking Wickets* and *Tricking the Batsman*, published in 1930 and 1934 respectively. Because these classic works have long been out of print, we believed this is an appropriate place to cite his thoughts on the great skills of bowling as a way to sum up and close this book.

GRIMMETT ON FLIGHT:

Grimmett may have been one of the first great bowlers to describe precisely what flight is, why bowlers use changes in flight to deceive the batsman, and why, according to his understanding, such deception is possible.

> *Flighting the ball is one of the bowler's little tricks by which he endeavours to mislead the batsman into thinking that the ball is going to pitch in a different place from that which was suggested by the early stages of its passage from the bowler's hand.*

This flighting of the ball is an endeavour to bowl it at different heights in the air, at the same time making it land in the same spot, or drop shorter than it appeared likely to do by its flight.

Why should this deceive the batsman, you will ask? If the ball is bowled higher in the air, has not the batsman more time to see the ball? And why is there a possibility that it will deceive him into thinking it will land in a different place?

This is easily explained…. Let us take a motor-car coming directly toward us. You will find it is difficult to gauge its speed. Now move to the side of it, so that it crosses at right-angles to you, and you will find it comparatively easy to judge its pace.

This is one reason why a ball thrown higher in the air is deceptive. At a certain part of its flight it is coming directly toward the batsman's eyes, and its pace is harder to judge. At the same time, a ball thrown high in the air is also coming at an unusual angle. It is not an ordinary delivery.

If, then, the height of the ball's trajectory is varied, it naturally follows that the part of its flight at which the ball is coming directly toward the eyes is different.

We, therefore, have a variation which… is valuable to a bowler. It will also be obvious that the longer the ball is in the air the more chance there is of some influence, such as spin or seam swerve, operating.

It is also necessary to bowl the ball slower, with increased height of trajectory, to allow for its dropping at a good length.

There is something curiously puzzling about a high dropping delivery, particularly a ball that has plenty of spin, and it will often play unexpected tricks.

A bowler who uses these devices will find it a great advantage to bowl into any breeze that may be blowing, as this helps to make the flight of the ball more deceptive (1934, pp. 79–81).

Grimmett did his homework, and saw things from the other side as well: he believed that stereoscopic vision – the use of both eyes at the same time – allowed batsmen to gain a better judgement of the distance, speed and angle of deliveries. In a rare moment of charity for his opponents, he urged batsmen to 'face the ball with both eyes at the same distance from it'. But as a bowler, he saw a chink: 'If a batsman has a one-eyed stance, don't forget to try him well out on the leg side. He is sure to be weak there' (1934, p. 139).

GRIMMETT ON LENGTH:

The leg-spinner was steadfast in his belief that it is the control of length that is the first crucial requirement for the successful bowler – and here his insights apply to all bowlers, not just the slow variety. He believed that young bowlers should be taught to bowl on a shortened pitch until they are strong enough to bowl a delivery of good length on a normal adult-sized pitch. We wholeheartedly endorse this view, which has been widely accepted by English cricket coaches.

Grimmett's advice on practising remains as fresh and useful as it was 70 years ago:

Let me tell you more about length…. Here is a simple method for young bowlers. It will help them to improve. Mark out a cricket pitch the correct length…. Now place a single stump at each end. At varying distance, to suit the particular type of bowler, pin a sheet of cardboard about three feet square on the spot where, as previously described, a good length ball would pitch.

You now have the stage set for an interesting practice or competition, taking in good length and direction.

Try to see how many times with a dozen balls you can hit the cardboard. You'll be surprised to find how really hard it is. There are few bowlers who can hit it consistently three times out of twelve. Yet, with conscientious practice, you will easily improve on this.

This is an interesting method of practice, and one which will appeal to all bowling aspirants, especially the youngsters (1934, pp. 42–43).

Coaches can't go wrong following this handy, low-tech advice. Remember that if cardboard is in short supply, or keeps being blown off the pitch, you can try the Woolmer variation and use a rubber car mat instead.

Grimmett, who continued to play international cricket until he was 44 years old, knew what he was talking about when he said:

Even when a bowler has lost his youth and power to break or swerve a ball, his ability to keep a good length will command respect from the best batsmen. Good length is everything. Without it no bowler will succeed.

A bowler who can retain a good length will reap a harvest of wickets on those days when he gets the assistance of a little rain or when he is on a crumbling wicket, and so will enjoy his cricket better than those who have neglected to lay a solid foundation in this respect (1934, pp. 44–45).

We hope that all bowlers (and their coaches) reading this book will find it a foundation from which to explore the many nuances of their crafts, whether it be the ferocity and strength that pace demands, the nagging persistence of the seamer, or the art of deception encompassed by spin. Whichever it is, never forget the mantra of all great bowlers: 'Practise, practise, practise!'

SELECT BIBLIOGRAPHY

Abernethy, B. 1982. 'Skill in cricket batting: Laboratory and applied evidence.' Proceedings of the Kinesiological Sciences Conference 7: 35–50.

Abernethy, B. and D.G. Russell. 1984. 'Advance cue utilisation by skilled cricket batsmen.' *Australian Journal of Science and Medicine in Sport* 16 (2): 2–10.

Aginsky, K.D., et al. 2008. 'The detection of a throw.' *British Journal of Sports Medicine* (in press).

Aginsky, K.D., L. Lategan et al. 2004. 'Shoulder injuries in provincial male fast bowlers – predisposing factors.' *Sports Medicine* 16 (1): 25–28.

Akram, Wasim (with Patrick Murphy). 1998. *Akram: The Biography of Wasim Akram*. London: Piatkus.

Alexander, S., D. Underwood and A.J. Cooke. 1998. 'Cricket glove design' in *The Engineering of Sport: Design and Development*, ed. S.J. Haake. Oxford: Blackwell Science.

Alfred, Luke. 2001. *Lifting the Covers: The Inside Story of South African Cricket*. Cape Town: Spearhead.

Allsopp, P.E. 2005. *Measuring Team Performance and Modelling the Home Advantage Effect in Cricket*. PhD dissertation, Swinburne University of Technology, Australia.

Allsopp, P.E. and S.R. Clarke. 2004. 'Rating teams and analysing outcomes in one-day and Test cricket.' *Journal of the Royal Statistical Society*: Series A 167 (4): 657.

Andrew, Keith. 1986. *Coaching Cricket*. Ramsbury: The Crowood Press.

Annear, P.T., T.M. Chakera et al. 1992. 'Pars interarticularis stress and disc degeneration in cricket's potent strike force: the fast bowler.' *Australia New Zealand Journal of Surgery* 62 (10): 768–773.

Arlott, John. 1949. *How to Watch Cricket*. London: Sporting Handbooks Ltd.

Arlott, John (ed.) 1972. *Cricket: The Great Captains*. Newton Abbot: The Sportsmans Book Club.

Australian Cricket Board. 2000. *Coaching Youth Cricket*. Human Kinetics.

Bahill, A.T. and T. LaRitz. 1984. 'Why can't batters keep their eyes on the ball?' *American Scientist* 72: 249–253.

Bartlett, R.M., N.P. Stockill et al. 1996. 'The biomechanics of fast bowling in men's cricket: A review.' *Journal of Sports Sciences* 14 (5): 403–424.

Barton, N.G. 1982. 'On the swing of a cricket ball in flight.' *Proceedings of the Royal Society of London: Series A* 379: 109–131.

Baum, Greg. 1996. 'What goes in to not getting out.' *The Good Weekend*, 21 December: 26–33.

Bawden, Mark and Ian Maynard. 2001. 'Towards an understanding of the personal experience of the "yips" in cricket.' *Journal of Sports Sciences* 19 (12): 937–53.

Bell-Jenje, T.C. and J. Gray. 2005. 'Incidence, nature and risk factors in shoulder injuries of national academy cricket players over 5 years – a retrospective study.' *South African Journal of Sports Medicine* 17 (4): 22–28.

Benaud, Richie. 1998. *Anything But … An Autobiography*. London: Hodder & Stoughton.

Botham, Ian (with Peter Hayter). 1995. *My Autobiography – Don't Tell Kath*. London: CollinsWillow.

Bown, W. and R. Mehta. 1993. 'The seamy side of swing bowling.' *New Scientist*: 21–24.

Bradman, Donald. 1958. *The Art of Cricket*. London: Hodder & Stoughton.

Brearley, Mike. 1985. *The Art of Captaincy*. London and Sydney: Hodder & Stoughton.

Broadstock, M. 1991. 'Sun protection at the cricket.' *Medical Journal of Australia* 154 (6): 430.

Brooks, R.D., R.W. Faff and D. Sokulsky. 2002. 'An ordered response model of Test cricket performance.' *Applied Economics* 34 (18).

Burnett, A.F., M.S. Khangure et al. 1996. 'Thoracolumbar disc degeneration in young fast bowlers in cricket: A follow-up study.' *Clinical Biomechanics* 11 (6): 305–310.

Campbell, F.W., S.E. Rothwell et al. 1987. 'Bad lights stops play.' *Ophthalmic & Physiological Optics: The Journal of the British College of Ophthalmic Opticians (Optometrists)* 7 (2): 165–67.

Cardus, Neville. 1929. *The Summer Game*. London: Grant Richards & Humphrey Toulmin.

Carter, M. and G. Guthrie. 2004. 'Cricket interruptus: Fairness and incentive in limited overs cricket matches.' *The Journal of the Operational Research Society* 55: 822–29.

Chappell, Greg. 2004. *Cricket: The Making of Champions*. South Melbourne: Lothian Books.

Cheetham, Jack. 1956. *I Declare*. Cape Town: Howard Timmins.

Christie, C.J., L. Todd and G.A. King. 2003. 'Energy cost of batting during a simulated cricket work bout.' In *Science and Medicine in Cricket*, eds. R.A. Stretch, T.D. Noakes and C.L. Vaughan, Second World Congress of Science and Medicine in Cricket.

Clarke, S.R. and P.E. Allsopp. 2001. 'Fair measures of performance: The World Cup of cricket.' *The Journal of the Operational Research Society* 52 (4): 471–79.

Clarke, S.R. and J.M. Norman. 1999. 'To run or not?: Some dynamic programming models in cricket.' *The Journal of the Operational Research Society* 50 (5): 536–545.

Clarke, S.R. and J.M. Norman. 2003. 'Dynamic programming in cricket: Choosing a night watchman.' *The Journal of the Operational Research Society* 54: 838–45.

Constantine, Learie (with C.L.R. James). 1933. *Cricket and I*. London: Allan.

Constantine, Learie (with Denzil Batchelor). 1966. *The Changing Face of Cricket*. London: Eyre & Spottiswoode.

Cook, Geoff and Neville Scott. 1991. *The Narrow Line: An Anatomy of Professional Cricket*. London: The Kingswood Press.

Cooke, J.C. 1955. 'The boundary layer and "seam" bowling.' *The Mathematical Gazette*: 196–99.

Daish, C.B. 1972. *The Physics of Ball Games*. London: The English Universities Press Ltd.

Davis, K. and B. Blanksby. 1976. 'A cinematographical analysis of fast bowling in cricket.' *Australian Journal for Health, Physical Education and Recreation* 71 (suppl.): 9–15.

Dellor, Ralph. 1990. *How to Coach Cricket*. London: Willow Books.

De Moore, G.M. 1999. 'The suicide of Thomas Wentworth Wills.' *Medical Journal of Australia* 171 (11–12): 656–58.

Dennis, R., P. Farhart et al. 2003. 'Bowling workload and the risk of injury in elite cricket fast bowlers.' *Journal of Science and Medicine in Sport* 6 (3): 359–367.

Dennis, R.J., C.F. Finch et al. 2005. 'Is bowling workload a risk factor for injury to Australian junior cricket fast bowlers?' *British Journal of Sports Medicine* 39 (11): 843–846.

De Silva, B.M. and T.B. Swartz. 1997. 'Winning the coin toss and the home team advantage in one-day international cricket matches.' *The New Zealand Statistician* 32: 16–22.

De Villiers, R.V., M. Pritchard et al. 2005. 'Scapular stress fracture in a professional cricketer and a review of the literature.' *South African Medical Journal* 95 (5): 312–317.

Donald, Allan (with Patrick Murphy). 2000. *White Lightning: The Autobiography*. Johannesburg: Jonathan Ball Publishers in conjunction with CollinsWillow.

Duckworth, F.C. and A.J. Lewis. 2004. 'A successful operational research intervention in one-day cricket.' *The Journal of the Operational Research Society* 55: 749–59.

Elliott, B. 2000. 'Back injuries and the fast bowler in cricket.' *Journal of Sports Sciences* 18 (12): 983–91.

Elliott, B., A. Burnett et al. 1995. 'The fast bowler in cricket: A sports medicine perspective.' *Sports Exercise and Injury* 1: 201–206.

Elliott, B., J.W. Davis et al. 1993. 'Disc degeneration and the young fast bowler in cricket.' *Clinical Biomechanics* 8: 227–234.

Elliot, B., D.H. Foster and S. Gray. 1986. 'Biomechanical and physical factors influencing fast bowling.' *Australian Journal of Science and Medicine in Sport* 18: 16–21.

Elliott, B., P. Hardcastle et al. 1992. 'The influence of fast bowling and physical factors on radiological features in high performance fast bowlers.' *Sports Medicine, Training and Rehabilitation* 3: 113–130.

Elliott, B. and M. Khangure. 2002. 'Disc degeneration and fast bowling in cricket: an intervention study.' *Medicine and Science in Sports and Exercise* 34 (11): 1 714–18.

Fingleton, J.H. 1946. *Cricket Crisis: Body Line and Other Lines*. Melbourne: Cassell & Co. Ltd.

Fletcher, J.G. 1955. 'Calories and cricket.' *Lancet* 268 (6 875): 1 165–66.

Foster, D., D. John et al. 1989. 'Back injuries to fast bowlers in cricket: a prospective study.' *British Journal of Sports Medicine* 23 (3): 150–154.

Francis, Tony. 1992. *The Zen of Cricket: Learning from Positive Thought*. London: Hutchinson.

Frith, David. 1990. *By His Own Hand: A Study of Cricket's Suicides*, republished as *Silence of the Heart: Cricket Suicides* in 2001. Edinburgh: Mainstream Publishers.

Fry, C.B. 1912. *Cricket (Batsmanship)*. London: Everleigh Nash & Co.

Gilfillan, T.C. and N. Nobandla. 2000. 'Modelling the performance of the South African national cricket team.' *South African Journal for Research in Sport, Physical Education and Recreation* 22 (1): 97–110.

Glazier, P.S., G.P. Paradisis et al. 2000. 'Anthropometric and kinematic influences on release speed in men's fast-medium bowling.' *Journal of Sports Sciences* 18 (12): 1 013–21.

Goddard, N. and D. Coull. 1994. 'Colour-blind cricketers and snowballs.' *British Medical Journal* 309 (6 970): 1 684–85.

Gore, C.J., P.C. Bourdon et al. 1993. 'Involuntary dehydration during cricket.' *International Journal of Sports Medicine* 14 (7): 387–95.

Goulet, C., C. Bard et al. 1989. 'Expertise Differences in Preparing to Return a Tennis Serve: A Visual Information Processing Approach.' *Journal of Sport and Exercise Psychology* 11: 382–98.

Gregory, P.L., M.E. Batt et al. 2002. 'Comparing injuries of spin bowling with fast bowling in young cricketers.' *Clinical Journal of Sports Medicine* 12 (2): 107–112.

Gregory, P.L., M.E. Batt et al. 2004. 'Is risk of fast bowling injury in cricketers greatest in those who bowl most? A cohort of young English fast bowlers.' *British Journal of Sports Medicine* 38 (2): 125–28.

Gregory, P.L., M.E. Batt et al. 2004. 'Comparing spondylolysis in cricketers and soccer players.' *British Journal of Sports Medicine* 38 (6): 737–742.

Grimmett, Clarence. 1934. *Tricking the Batsman*. London: Hodder & Stoughton.

Guha, Ramachandra. 1994. *Spin and Other Turns*. New Delhi and London: Penguin.

Hardcastle, P.H. 1993. 'Repair of spondylolysis in young fast bowlers.' *Journal of Bone and Joint Surgery (British Volume)* 75 (3): 398–402.

Hardcastle, P., P. Annear et al. 1992. 'Spinal abnormalities in young fast bowlers.' *Journal of Bone and Joint Surgery (British Volume)* 74 (3): 421–425.

Hoberman, J. 1992. *Mortal Engines: The Science of Performance and the Dehumanization of Sport*. New York: The Free Press.

Holmes, Richard. 2003. *Acts of War: The Behaviour of Men in Battle*. London: Weidenfeld & Nicholson.

Hughes, Simon. 1997. *A Lot of Hard Yakka*. London: Headline.

Hughes, Simon. 2001. *Jargonbusting: The Analyst's Guide to Test Cricket*. London: Channel Four Books / Macmillan.

Humphries, D. and M. Jamison. 2004. 'Clinical and magnetic resonance imaging features of cricket bowler's side strain.' *British Journal of Sports Medicine* 38 (5): E21.

Hurrion, P.D., R. Dyson et al. 2000. 'Simultaneous measurement of back and front foot ground reaction forces during the same delivery stride of the fast-medium bowler.' *Journal of Sports Sciences* 18 (12): 993–97.

James, C.L.R. 1963, 1994. *Beyond A Boundary*. London: Serpent's Tail.

Johnstone, P.G. 2003. '"Sledging" – the practice of psychological distraction in cricket.' In *Science and Medicine in Cricket*, eds. R.A. Stretch, T.D. Noakes and C.L. Vaughan, Second World Congress of Science and Medicine in Cricket.

Kantor, Brian. 2007. 'A statistical analysis of the World Cup 2007.' Investec Newsletter 11 May.

Keri, J., et al. 2006. *Baseball Between the Numbers*. New York: Basic Books.

Kimber, A.C. and A.R. Hansford. 1993. 'A statistical analysis of batting in cricket.' *Journal of the Royal Statistical Society Series A: Statistics in Society* 156 (3): 443–55.

Kirk, D., T. Carlson et al. 1997. 'The economic impact on families of children's participation in junior sport.' *Australian Journal of Science and Medicine in Sport* 29 (2): 27–33.

Knott, Alan. 1977. *Wicket-keeping*. London: Stanley Paul.

Lamb, Allan (with Jack Bannister). 1997. *Allan Lamb: My Autobiography*. London: CollinsWillow.

Land, M.F. and P. McLeod. 2000. 'From eye movements to actions: how batsmen hit the ball.' *Nature Neuroscience* 3 (12): 1 340–45.

Lara, Brian (with Brian Scovell). 1994. *Brian Lara: Beating the Field*. London: Partridge Press.

Lewis, Michael. 2003. *Moneyball: The Art of Winning an Unfair Game*. New York: W.W. Norton & Company.

Lewis, Tony. 1994. *MCC Masterclass: The New MCC Coaching Book*. London: Weidenfeld & Nicolson.

Lillee, Dennis. 1982. *The Art of Fast Bowling*. Guilford, Surrey: Lutterworth Press.

Lillee, Dennis (with Bob Harris). 2003. *Lillee: An Autobiography*. Sydney: Hodder.

Lloyd, D.G, J. Alderson and B.C. Elliot. 2000. 'A upper limb kinamatic for the examination of cricket bowling: A case study of Muttiah Muralitharan.' *Journal of Sports Sciences* 18: 975–82.

Lyttleton, R.A. 1957. 'The swing of a cricket ball.' *Cricket Journal*: 186–191.

Marshall, R. and R. Ferdinands. 2003. 'The effect of a flexed elbow on bowling speed in cricket.' *Sports Biomechanics* 2 (1): 65–71.

Martin-Jenkins, Christopher. 1996. *World Cricketers: A Biographical Dictionary*. Oxford: Oxford University Press.

May, Peter. 1956. *Peter May's Book of Cricket*. London: Cassell and Company Ltd.

McLeod, Peter. 1987. 'Visual reaction time and high speed ball games.' *Perception* 16 (1): 49–59.

Mehta, R.D. 1985. 'Aerodynamics of sports balls.' *Annual Review of Fluid Mechanics* 17: 151–189.

Mehta, R.D. and D. Wood. 1980. 'Aerodynamics of the cricket ball.' *New Scientist*: 442–47.

Mehta, R.D, K. Bentley et al. 1983. 'Factors affecting cricket ball swing.' *Nature* 303 (30 June 1983): 787–88.

Milburn, P.D. and G. Nuttridge. 1999. *The Nature, Prevalence and Risk Factors Associated with Pace Bowling Injuries in Men's Cricket*. Wellington: Sports Science New Zealand Technical Report.

Millson, H.B., J. Gray et al. 2004. 'Dissociation between back pain and bone stress reaction as measured by CT scan in young cricket fast bowlers.' *British Journal of Sports Medicine* 38 (5): 586–591.

Noakes, T.D. 2006. 'Laboratory research, commercial interests and advice to the public on fluid ingestion during exercise: The development of a fatal foundation myth.' *Clinical Journal of Sport Medicine* (submitted).

Noakes, T.D. 2003. 'Overconsumption of fluids by athletes.' *British Medical Journal* 327 (7 407): 113–114.

Noakes, T.D. 2003. *Lore of Running* (4th edition). Cape Town: Oxford University Press.

Noakes, T.D., N. Goodwin et al. 2005. 'Water intoxication: a possible complication during endurance exercise.' *Wilderness and Environmental Medicine* 16 (4): 221–27.

Noakes, T.D. and S. Granger. 1995. *Running Your Best*. Cape Town: Oxford University Press.

Noakes, T.D. and A. St Clair Gibson. 2004. 'Logical limitations to the "catastrophe" models of fatigue during exercise in humans.' *British Journal of Sports Medicine* 38 (5): 648–49.

Noakes, T.D., A. St Clair Gibson et al. 2004. 'From catastrophe to complexity: a novel model of integrative central neural regulation of effort and fatigue during exercise in humans.' *British Journal of Sports Medicine* 38 (4): 511–14.

Noakes, T.D., A. St Clair Gibson et al. 2005. 'From catastrophe to complexity: a novel model of integrative central neural regulation of effort and fatigue during exercise in humans: summary and conclusions.' *British Journal of Sports Medicine* 39 (2): 120–24.

Nummela, A.T., K.A. Heath et al. 2008. 'Fatigue during a 5-km running time trial.' *International Journal of Sports Medicine* (in press).

Orchard, J., T. James et al. 2002. 'Injuries in Australian cricket at first-class level 1995/1996 to 2000/2001.' *British Journal of Sports Medicine* 36 (4): 270–74.

Oslear, Don and Jack Bannister. 1996. *Tampering With Cricket*. London: CollinsWillow.

Peebles, Ian. 1969. *Straight From the Shoulder: 'Throwing' – its History and Cure*. Newton Abbot: The Sportsmans Book Club.

Penrose, J.M.T. and N.K. Roach. 1995. 'Decision-making and advanced cue utilisation by cricket batsmen.' *Journal of Human Movement Studies* 29: 199–218.

Philpott, Peter. 1995. *The Art of Wrist-spin Bowling*. Ramsbury: The Crowood Press.

Portus, M.R., B.R. Mason et al. 2003. 'Fast bowling arm actions and the illegal delivery law in men's high performance cricket matches.' In *Science and Medicine in Cricket*, eds. R.A. Stretch, T.D. Noakes and C.L. Vaughan, Second World Congress of Science and Medicine in Cricket.

Portus, M.R., P.J. Sinclair et al. 2000. 'Cricket fast bowling performance and technique and the influence of selected physical factors during an 8-over spell.' *Journal of Sports*

Sciences 18 (12) 999–1 011.

Potter, Jack and Ashley Mote. 2001. *The Winning Edge: The Secrets and Techniques of the World's Best Cricketers.* Manchester: The Parrs Wood Press.

Pyke, F.S., G.C. Crouch et al. 1975. *The Testing and Training of an International Fast Bowler – Dennis Lillee.* Western Australia.

Ranawat, V.S., J.K. Dowell et al. 2003. 'Stress fractures of the lumbar pars interarticularis in athletes: a review based on long-term results of 18 professional cricketers.' *Injury* 34 (12): 915–919.

Ranjitsinhji, K.S. 1897. *The Jubilee Book of Cricket.* Edinburgh and London: William Blackwood.

Regan, D. 1992. 'Visual judgements and misjudgements in cricket, and the art of flight.' *Perception* 21 (1): 91–115.

Regan, D. 1997. 'Visual factors in hitting and catching.' *Journal of Sports Sciences* 15 (6): 533–58.

Reilly, T. and D. Chana. 1994. 'Spinal shrinkage in fast bowling.' *Ergonomics* 37 (1): 127–32.

Renshaw, I. and M.M. Fairweather. 2000. 'Cricket bowling deliveries and the discrimination ability of professional and amateur batters.' *Journal of Sports Sciences* 18 (12): 951–57.

Richards, Viv (with Bob Harris). 2000. *Sir Vivian: The Definitive Autobiography.* London: Michael Joseph.

Riley, Pat. 1994. *The Winner Within: A Life Plan for Team Players.* Berkley Trade.

Ripoll, H. and P. Fleurance. 1988. 'What does keeping one's eye on the ball mean?' *Ergonomics* 31 (11): 1 647–54.

Rundell, Michael. 1996. *The Dictionary of Cricket.* Oxford: Oxford University Press.

Sharwood, K.A., M. Collins et al. 2004. 'Weight changes, medical complications, and performance during an Ironman triathlon.' *British Journal of Sports Medicine* 38 (6): 718–724.

Scarf, P. and X. Shi. 2005. 'Modelling match outcomes and decision support for setting a final innings target in test cricket.' *IMA Journal of Management Mathematics* 16 (2): 161–78.

Shillinglaw, A.L. 2003. *Bradman Revisited: The Legacy of Sir Donald Bradman.* Manchester: The Parrs Wood Press.

Simpson, Bob (with Terry Brindle). 1996. *The Reasons Why.* Sydney: HarperSports.

Snow, John (with Kenneth Wheeler). 1968. *The Art of Bowling.* London: Stanley Paul.

Sobers, Garfield (with Ivo Tennant). 1996. *Sobers: The Changing Face of Cricket.* London: Ebury Press.

St Clair Gibson, A., E.V. Lambert et al. 2001. 'Exercise and fatigue-control mechanisms.' *International Journal of Sports Medicine* 2 (3): 1–14.

Stretch, R.A., G. Barnard et al. 2002. 'Improving the accuracy and consistency of shot reproduction in cricket batting through a vision training programme.' *The South African Optometrist* 61 (4): 145–150.

Stretch, R.A. 2003. 'Cricket injuries: a longitudinal study of the nature of injuries to South African cricketers.' *British Journal of Sports Medicine* 37 (3): 250–253.

Stretch, R.A., R. Bartlett et al. 2000. 'A review of batting in men's cricket.' *Journal of Sports Sciences* 18 (12): 931–49.

Stretch, R.A., T. Botha et al. 2003. 'Back injuries in young fast bowlers: A radiological investigation of the healing of spondylolysis and pedicle sclerosis.' *South African Medical Journal* 93 (8): 611–616.

Stretch, R.A., E. du Toit et al. 1998. 'The force absorption characteristics of cricket batting pads at four impact velocities.' *Sports Medicine* (October 1998): 9–13.

Stretch, Richard and Janine Gray. 1998. *Fast Bowling Injury Prevention.* United Cricket Board of South Africa.

Stretch, Richard, Tim Noakes, Mike Proctor and Clive Rice. 1997. *Fast Bowling Injury Prevention Strategy.* United Cricket Board of South Africa.

Stretch, R.A. and J. Tyler. 1995. 'The force absorption characteristics of cricket batting gloves at four impact velocities.' *Sports Medicine* (September 1995): 22–29.

Stretch, R.A., J.V. von Hagen et al. 2000. 'The effect of fencamfamine on the accuracy and consistency of shot reproduction in cricket batting.' *Sports Medicine* (November 2000): 21–25.

Swartz, T.B., P.S. Gill et al. 2006. 'Optimal batting orders in one-day cricket.' *Comparative and Operational Research* 33: 1939–50.

Synge, Allen and Derek Anns. 1987. *Masterstrokes.* London: The Kingswood Press.

Tainton, Neil and John Klug. 2002. *The Cricket Pitch and its Outfield.* Pietermaritzburg: University of Natal Press.

Tucker, R., L. Rauch et al. 2004. 'Impaired exercise performance in the heat is associated with an anticipatory reduction in skeletal muscle recruitment.' *Pflugers Archive* 448 (4): 422–430.

Turner, Matthew. 2002. *The Motion of Balls in Sports.* Dept of Mathematics, University of East Anglia.

Tyson, Frank. 1977. *Complete Cricket Coaching.* London: Pelham Books Ltd.

Wallis, R., B. Elliott et al. 2002. 'The effect of a fast bowling harness in cricket: An intervention study.' *Journal of Sports Sciences* 20 (6): 495–506.

Warne, Shane (with Mark Ray). 1997. *My Own Story.* London: Bookman Projects Ltd.

Waugh, Steve. 1995. *Steve Waugh's West Indies Tour Diary.* Sydney: HarperSports.

Webster, F.A.M. 1948. *The Science of Athletics.* London: Nicholas Kaye.

Wilde, Simon. 1994. *Letting Rip: The Fast-bowling Threat from Lillee to Waqar.* London: H.F. & G. Witherby.

Williams, Charles. 1997. *Bradman: An Australian Hero.* London: Abacus.

Woolmer, Bob. 1984. *Bob Woolmer: Pirate and Rebel? An Autobiography.* London: Arthur Barker Ltd.

Woolmer, Bob. 1993. *Skilful Cricket.* London: A & C Black.

Woolmer, Bob (with Ivo Tennant). 2000. *Woolmer on Cricket.* London: Virgin Publishing Ltd.

INDEX

Note: page numbers in *italic* refer to illustrations or examples.

accuracy and rhythm 20–1, 37–9, 89

Adams, Paul 19, 86, 88, 109

aerodynamics

of spin 92, 101–7, *102, 103, 104, 106*

of swing 69–81, *70, 71, 73, 74, 75, 77, 78, 79,* 83–4, *84*

Afridi, Shahid 34

Aginsky, Kerith 28–33

Ahmed, Mushtaq 86, 113, 115

aiming the ball 45

air friction/flow 69–77

Akhtar, Shoaib 18, 23

Akram, Wasim 4, 11, 13, 17–18, 50, 82, 83

Alderman, Terry 45

Ambrose, Curtley 46

armpits, use of 55

art of deceit 90–1

The Art of Wrist spin Bowling (Philpott) 119

Atherton, Michael 62

athleticism 49

attributes of

fast bowlers 48–50

medium-paced bowlers 47–8

slow bowlers 87

balance 9

'Ball of the Century' 19, 105–7, *106*

ball swing

height of seam 78–80, *78, 79*

make of ball 82–3

speed of delivery 80, *84*

vertical axis and 81

weather and 81–2

wind speed 80

ball tampering 61–2

baseball, difference to cricket 22–3

basic action 8–45

bowling off the wrong foot 12–13, *13,* 19–20

line and length 40–5, 120–1

mixed action 11–12

rhythm and accuracy 20–1, 37–9, 89

the run up 9, *9,* 14–22, *16*

throwing 22–37

beamer 43–4

Bedi, Bishen 34, 85

Bedser, Sir Alec 46, 82

Benaud, Richie 87, 109, 114

Bevan, Michael 109

boots, for fast bowlers 66–8

Bosanquet, B.J.T 111

Botha, Johan 29, 32, 33

Botham, Ian 47, 59, 61, 69, 83

bouncer 42

boundary layer 73–5, *77*

'bowling downhill' 10

bowling off the wrong foot 12–13, *13,* 19–20

Bradman, Sir Donald 116

captains, being supportive of bowlers 38

'carrying angle' 28–33, *28, 29, 31*

Chandana, Upul 86

children, coaching of 5, 11, 12, 14–15, 16, 24, 38–9, 51, 68, 113

chucking 23, 24–7

clothing, for fast bowlers 68

coaching younger players 5, 11, 12, 14–15, 16, 24, 38–9, 51, 68, 113

Cronje, Hansie 62

'cruising time' 18

cutter ball 63–5, *64, 65*

deceit, art of 90–1

deliveries *10,* 10, **51–68,** 80, *84,* 92–100

determination 50

Donald, Allan 4, 9, 18, 19, 48, 49, 54

doosra 34, 103, 115

Drakes, Vasbert 17

elbow, bending of 24–37, *26, 27, 31, 35*

fast bowling 46–84, 90

attributes 48–50

deliveries 19, 51–68

grip *51*

aerodynamics of swing 69–84

troubleshooting 54, 63

finger spin 85, 93–7, *94, 96, 100*

flight 91, 119–20

Flintoff, Andrew 47

flipper ball 114

'floater' ball 94–5

follow through *10,* 10

Fraser, Angus 62

front-on action 10–11, 98–9, *98*

full toss 43

the gather 9

Gatting, Mike 105, 107

good length 43

googly 111–13, *112*

Gough, Darren 48, 60

Griffin, Geoff 23

Grimmett, Clarrie 66, 102, 109, 114,
119–21

grip 60, 64, 94, 110, 112–13
    cutters *64*, 64, *65*
    finger-spin *94*, 94, 96
    googly *112*, *112*
    inswingers *58*, 58, 59, *59*
    leg-spin 110, *110*, *111*
    medium-/fast-pace bowling *51*
    outswingers *57*, 57
    reverse swing 60
    seam bowling *52*, 52

Hadlee, Richard 18, 19, 37, 66

Hair, Darrell 34, 61, 62

half-volley 43

Hall, Wesley 14, 46

Harper, Roger 85

Healy, Ian 118

height 48–9

Henderson, Claude 20

high arm 99–100

history of bowling 5–7

Hobbs, Sir Jack 116

Hobson, Denys 112

Hogg, Brad 109

Hoggard, Matthew 82

Holding, Michael 14, 46, 48

inswingers 58–9, *58*, *59*

International Cricket Council (ICC) 25,
27, 28, 34–5

Khan, Imran 47, 59, 62, 69, 83

Khan, Moin 115

kit, for fast bowlers 66–8

Klusener, Lance 68

'knuckle ball' 114

Kumble, Anil 19, 86, 113

Lamb, Allan 59

Lara, Brian 4

Larwood, Harold 48

The Law, changes to 6, 24–6

Lee, Brett 23, 45, *45*

left-handedness 109

leg cutter ball *64*, 64, *65*

leg-spin *104*, 108–15, *110*, *111*, 119

length 40–4, *41*, *45*, 120–1

Lewis, Rawl 86

Lillee, Dennis 19, 37–38, 47, 50, 56, 81

limited-overs 7, 44

Lindwall, Ray 48

line 40, 44–5, *44*, *45*

long hop 42

losing the rhythm 37–8

McGrath, Glenn 41, *41*, 44, 45, *45*, 49,
50, 53

Magnus Effect 101–7, *102*

Malcolm, Devon 46

Mallet, Ashley 91

Marshall, Malcolm 11

Massie, Bob 56

May, Tim 85

medium-pace bowling 46–84
    attributes 47–8
    deliveries 51–68
    grip *51*
    aerodynamics of swing 69–84
    troubleshooting 54, 63

Mehta, Dr Rabi 83

mixed action 11–12

momentum 9, 15, 16, 17, 51

Muralitharan, Muttiah 4, 23, 25, 26, 28,
29, 32, 33, 34–7, *35*, *36*, 86, 88,
98, 99, 115

Mushtaq, Saqlain 100, 115

Nawaz, Sarfraz 59

Ngam, Mfuneko 54

Ntini, Makhaya 46

off-cutter ball, *64*, 64, *65*

off spinners 97, *97*, *104*

one-day cricket 85

O'Reilly, Bill 119

outswingers 57–8, *57*

Pakistan 53, 59, 61–2, 83–4

Philpott, Peter 38, 113, 119

playing conditions, adapting to 21–2

Pollock, Shaun 49

Portus, Marc 26–7

positioning 7

practising
    accuracy 39
    medium-/fast-pace bowling 66

Price, John 14

Price, Ray 86

Proctor, Mike 12, 14

Qadir, Abdul 4, 85, 112

Ramadhin, Sonny 115

Ramnarine, Dinanath 86

reverse swing bowling 59–62, 83–4

Reynolds' number 75–7, 77, 80

rhythm and accuracy 20–1, 37–9, 89

Richards, Sir Vivian 116

round arm 99–100

the run up 9, *9*, 14–22, *16*

Schofield, Chris 86

Schwarz, Reg 111–12

seam

    angle of 81

    height of 78–80, *78*, *79*

    vertical axis and 81

seam bowling 17, 52–4, *52*, *53*, 90

the set up 9, *9*

short of a length 42

side-on action 10–11, 98

Singh, Harbhajan 26, 34

slow bowling 85–121

    art of deceit 90–1

    attributes 87

    deliveries 92–100

    spin 88–9, 101–18

Snow, John 8, 9, 10, 20, 37, 47

Sobers, Sir Garfield (Garry) 14, 116

South Africa 53, 55, 86, 111

speed 20–1

spin, aerodynamics of 92, 101–7, *102*,

    103, *104*, *106*

spin bowling 19–20, 86

    art of deceit 90–1

    attributes 88, 89

    Clarrie Grimmett on 119–21

    elbow flexion/extension 33

    family tree *92*

    finger-spin 85, 93–7, *94*, *96*, *100*

    one-day cricket and 85

    variations 114

Statham, Brian 45

Strang, Paul 86

strength 49

suppleness 48

swing bowling 55–63, 90

    aerodynamics of 70–81, *70*, *71*, *73*,

    74, *75*, *77*, *78*, *79*, 83–4, *84*

Symcox, Pat 55

Taking Wickets (Grimmett) 119

tampering with the ball 61–2

Tanvir, Sohail 13

target bowling 39

Tendulkar, Sachin 4

Thomson, Jeff 48

throwing 22–37

timing 9

top spinner 103, *103*

Tricking the Batsman (Philpott) 119–20,

    121

trouble-shooting

    medium-/fast-pace bowling 54, 63

    seam bowling 54

    swing-related problems 63

    'wrong-footedness' 12–13, *13*, 19–20

Trueman, Fred 45, 48

Tufnell, Phil 85

turbulent flow 72–3, *77*

Turner, Matthew 81–2

20-over cricket 7

Tyson, Frank 46

under-cutter ball 100

Underwood, Derek 14, 85

the unfold 9, *9*

vertical axis and ball swing 81

Vogler, Albert 111–12

Walker, Max 12–13

Walsh, Courtney 53

Warne, Shane 4, 15, 19, 85, 88, **105–7**,

    114, 115, **116–18**, *117*

Waugh, Mark 114

weather conditions 21, 80, 81–2, 95

weight 49

West India 42, 46, 47, 86

Willis, Bob 48

Willsher, Ned 6

wind conditions 21, 80

wind resistance 71

'wobble' 24

work ethic 50

Wright, Doug 19

wrist-spin 93, 104, 116–18, *117*, 119

'wrong-footed' bowling 12–13, *13*, 19–20

yorker 43

Younis, Waqar 11, 47, 60, 82

youth and age 50